Editor
Lorin E. Klistoff, M.A.

Cover Artist
Marilyn Goldberg

Editor in Chief
Karen J. Goldfluss, M.S. Ed.

Art Production Manager
Kevin Barnes

Imaging
Leonard P. Swierski

Publisher

Mary D. Smith, M.S. Ed.

GRADE 5

VOCABULARY
PUZZLES & ACTIVITIES

Building vocabulary skills one puzzle at a time!

Author

Nancy P. Sibtain

Teacher Created Resources, Inc.
6421 Industry Way
Westminster, CA 92683
www.teachercreated.com
ISBN: 978-1-4206-8077-5
© 2008 Teacher Created Res
Made in U.S.A.

Teacher Created Resources

▫▫▫▫ Table of Contents ▫▫▫▫

Table of Contents

Introduction

Vocabulary Puzzles & Activities (Grade 5) is a challenging and fun way for children to improve their spelling, vocabulary, knowledge of synonyms, and grammar.

About the Book

The book is divided into three levels (Level A = Beginning, Level B = Intermediate, and Level C = Advanced). Students can, of course, move up or down the levels according to their needs. The clues for each crossword puzzle consist of three parts: the number of the square in which the word starts, the clue, and then a number in parentheses to tell the solver how many letters are in the solution word. (*Note:* If the number of letters shown in parentheses is, for example, (3, 3), it means that there are two words in the solution, each with three letters, e.g., "set off." The solution must be written in the crossword without a space between the words.)

Each crossword page also includes other activities to add to the enjoyment. The section "Find the Words" gives students a chance to find some words from the crossword puzzle in a word search. Anagrams can be made by scrambling and rearranging the letters of a word to form another word or words (e.g., CANED is an anagram of DANCE). There are also activities that include hidden words, breaking codes, words in words, and much more!

In the back of the book, there is a word list that includes all the words used in the puzzles. Incorporate the words into your everyday classroom activities. For example, for each week, create a word list and activities from the words in a puzzle. Categorize by vowel sounds, syllabication rules, parts of speech, etc. Be creative!

Helpful Hints for Students

The best method for students to start a puzzle is to look through all the clues until they find one with a solution they know. This may be an across-word or a down-word. Once a student has written in the word in the correct space, the next step is to look at the clue for a word that crosses it, because one of the letters is given. Remind students that sometimes a word which seems to be the obvious and correct solution can turn out to be the wrong one. Also, encourage them to use the Internet as a resource when solving clues.

Let students know that when solving crossword puzzles, they do not need to start with the first clue. Sometimes two meanings, separated by a semicolon, are given in a clue to help the solver (e.g., Most plants have these; goes away from). A group of dashes is sometimes used in a clue where it is difficult to supply a synonym or other description. For example, the clue might be as follows: Dad picked me up from school in his – – – (3). The solution would be "car"—the number of dashes indicates the number of letters in the solution. An answer key for all puzzles is located on pages 56–61.

Tell students that it is important to carefully read the clue, especially in terms of the tense of the verb required. A clue that directs them to the word "saw" will clearly show that the past tense, not the present tense "see," is required. The same applies to the number. If the clue requires a plural word, a word in the singular will be the wrong word—even though it fits. For example, the clue might be as follows: Many people sit at these when they write (5). The solution will be "desks"; it could not be "table" because the clue asks for a plural word of five letters.

Have students use pencils for crossword-problem solving. Have them keep an eraser nearby, so they can easily erase an incorrect answer.

Overall, solving crossword puzzles is an enjoyable and stimulating activity that children can take with them into their adult lives. The completion of a puzzle can bring to child and adult alike that sense of achievement that we all need to experience from time to time. Good luck!

Level A Unit 1

(Answers on page 56)

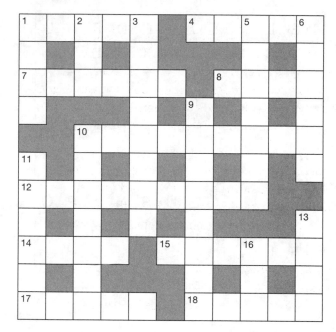

Find the Words

All ten of the <u>down-words</u> in the crossword are hidden in this square, some running across and some running down. Can you find all of them?

S	O	M	T	E	H	U	Y	A	I	R
E	M	E	R	A	L	D	X	P	U	K
N	C	C	I	F	G	W	A	Z	L	E
C	O	S	T	L	R	I	K	O	B	T
H	F	M	M	T	N	G	R	I	P	T
T	W	I	F	R	H	W	E	Z	K	L
E	O	L	U	E	U	A	L	O	F	E
A	N	E	M	K	R	M	F	W	A	C
F	E	S	L	I	P	S	T	I	C	K
U	T	T	O	B	U	K	O	M	N	I
B	R	E	A	K	E	R	S	U	F	E

Across

1. Move forward on hands and knees (5)
4. Talk (5)
7. Little bits of leftover food or cloth (6)
8. The smallest money unit; one-hundredth of a dollar (4)
10. Water pouring down from high rocks (9)
12. In stories, a fairy or a wizard carries this (5,4)
14. Jump high (4)
15. The middle point of anything (6)
17. A girl's name (5)
18. A large, hungry fish that frightens humans (5)

Down

1. The price of something (4)
2. This goes into our lungs when we breathe in (3)
3. Something used to color the lips (8)
5. Some rings have this green stone (7)
6. We boil water in a jug or a – – – – – – (6)
9. Big waves that turn into foam when they reach the shore (8)
10. Native Americans used to live in these (7)
11. Expressions on faces showing happiness (6)
13. A trip or journey; Star – – – – (4)
16. A drink (3)

Anagram

An anagram is the scrambling and rearranging of the letters of a word to make a new word. The three words below can be rearranged to make a word in the crossword.

FAR ALL WET _____

Name _____

Date _____

Level A — Unit 2
(Answers on page 56)

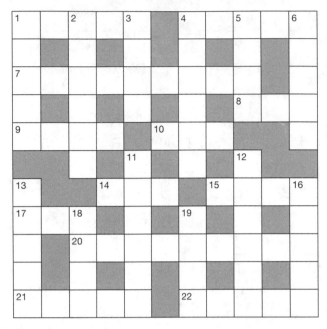

Find the Words

All the <u>across-words</u> in the crossword are in this square. Can you find all twelve of them?

B	L	I	M	H	A	R	D	F	H	U
U	C	D	O	O	V	X	P	L	I	M
S	W	I	T	C	S	T	Y	W	P	P
B	A	C	L	T	O	S	N	I	V	Y
L	A	T	E	R	R	F	E	A	S	T
U	B	A	X	U	F	L	P	R	Y	D
A	F	T	E	R	N	O	O	N	T	R
R	B	I	H	G	U	R	N	I	P	O
Y	E	O	F	W	A	T	C	H	Y	P
E	L	N	R	I	S	R	L	O	H	I
S	X	I	E	L	O	M	I	S	E	R

Across

1 A large meal, usually cooked to celebrate something (5)

4 Observe; we may wear this on one wrist (5)

7 A school or home exercise in which we must write down the words that are read or said to us (9)

8 A short reply to indicate agreement (3)

9 Allow to fall (4)

10 An inflamed swelling on the eyelid (3)

14 A form of public transportation (3)

15 Difficult; not soft (4)

17 You swing this part of your body when you dance (3)

20 The time between midday and evening (9)

21 At a future time (5)

22 Someone who hoards money and doesn't like spending it on anything (5)

Down

1 Having lost some or all of its color (5)

2 A heavy object dropped over the side of a boat so that it won't move (6)

3 An amphibian which is like a frog but bigger (4)

4 The parts of our arms which are closest to our hands (6)

5 Extremely small (4)

6 A pet animal that you can ride (5)

11 This is usually spread on bread (6)

12 Known about by very many people (6)

13 Another word for "will" (5)

16 You are called this when you donate blood (5)

18 A formal agreement between groups or countries (4)

19 To decorate with; – – – – the Christmas tree (4)

Anagram

Find the word in the crossword that has the anagram DO TITANIC.

_____

Name _____

Date _____

 **Level A** # Unit 3
(Answers on page 56)

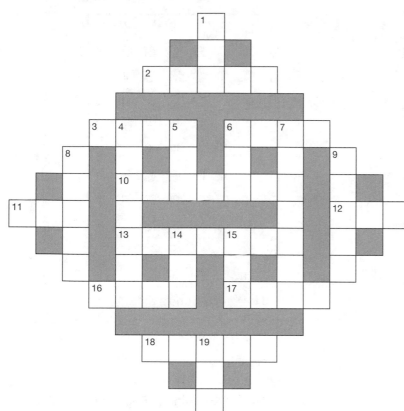

Across

2 A fruit (5)

3 A place where items are bought (4)

6 Tea and coffee are usually served in these (4)

10 Kitchen device for making bread hot and brown on the surface (7)

11 Male sheep (3)

12 Female sheep (3)

13 Natural environment for a living thing (7)

16 Requests (4)

17 Simple; not difficult (4)

18 We use this to dry ourselves (5)

Down

1 Not an adult dog but a – – – (3)

4 Chests or cupboards with shelves for storage (7)

5 This grows with others in a pod (3)

6 A household pet (3)

7 Those who attack and rob ships at sea (7)

8 More than one young sheep (5)

9 Lambs which have grown up (5)

14 A form of public transportation (3)

15 This may be worn around the neck with a shirt that has a collar (3)

19 The opposite of dry (3)

Find the Words

The ten <u>across-words</u> in the crossword are hidden in the square. Can you find all of them?

S	P	H	R	E	T	O	W	E	L	T
O	L	A	S	K	S	D	R	X	O	O
L	U	P	T	E	R	R	A	M	V	A
K	N	P	Y	R	A	L	V	U	M	S
I	D	L	O	C	E	W	E	T	R	T
H	L	E	A	S	Y	G	E	O	L	E
W	E	M	B	A	S	M	P	F	R	R
S	R	I	R	F	H	B	R	E	E	K
H	A	B	I	T	A	T	I	L	C	R
O	G	O	V	R	D	K	L	N	H	O
P	H	L	T	U	C	U	P	S	I	F

Anagram

Find the word in the crossword that has the anagram ROTATES.

_____

Level A — Unit 4
(Answers on page 56)

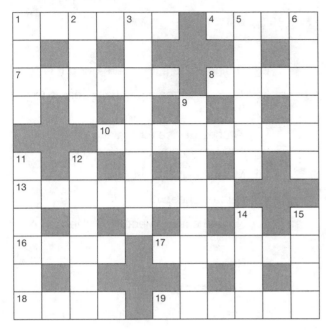

Across

1. Nearly; not quite (6)
4. Fifty percent (4)
7. Masses of white mist which we see in the sky (6)
8. A big member of the cat family (4)
10. Large fish-eating waterbirds with very big bills (8)
13. Little books (8)
16. Do what one is told to do (4)
17. A juicy fruit (6)
18. The entrance in a fence (4)
19. A container made of cardboard (6)

Anagram

Find the word in the crossword which has the anagram IN PLACES.

_____

Find the Words

There are eight six-letter words in the crossword. All of them are hidden in this small square.

O	B	L	O	N	G	V	I	T
F	L	U	C	E	L	G	B	R
I	A	B	A	L	M	O	S	T
N	C	I	R	G	E	R	W	U
I	L	P	T	R	S	A	I	H
S	O	F	O	I	B	N	J	E
H	U	I	N	B	G	G	I	P
O	D	K	F	O	R	E	S	T
F	S	W	A	N	I	M	A	L

Down

1. The curved part under one's foot (4)
2. The satellite of our Earth that shines at night (4)
3. Quickly, when we didn't expect it (8)
5. Any living creature which is not a plant (6)
6. Complete or end whatever we are doing (6)
9. The name of former Queen of England (8)
11. Another word for a rectangle (6)
12. Large area of land where there are many trees (6)
14. This is made when two pieces of string are tied together firmly (4)
15. This is the prettiest picture I have ever – – – – (4)

Words from Words

The solution to 17-across has only six letters, but you will be surprised to learn that at least sixteen words, of three letters or more, can be made from those six letters. See how many you can find. A score between 7 and 10 is good.

_____

_____

_____

Name _____

Date _____

Unit 5

(Answers on page 56)

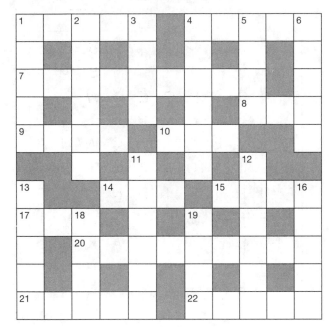

Across

1. Below; beneath (5)
4. To use a broom (5)
7. When we are away from our friends, we can use this to talk to them (9)
8. Move the head slightly to show that we agree with another person (3)
9. Bread shaped and baked in one piece (4)
10. The first counting number (3)
14. A young bear or a young wolf (3)
15. The main cook in a restaurant (4)
17. A statement which is not true (3)
20. We can write stories, play games, and send e-mails using these (9)
21. An ingredient used in making bread or cakes (5)
22. Very tall plants with trunks and branches (5)

Down

1. We must remain in the classroom – – – – – we hear the bell (5)
2. This consists of 100 cents (6)
3. When fruit is ready to be eaten, we say it is this (4)
4. We use these when we eat soup (6)

Find the Words

All the <u>down-words</u> in the crossword are hidden in this square.

E	W	A	L	F	T	O	S	P	A	G
M	I	U	O	S	U	M	M	E	R	I
A	Y	N	D	A	N	P	I	Y	D	E
U	N	T	I	L	S	H	U	M	G	V
S	A	K	F	N	D	O	L	L	A	R
C	H	E	V	E	M	P	S	F	B	E
H	O	C	G	V	U	A	R	I	P	E
E	M	L	R	E	P	N	O	S	O	C
E	B	I	U	N	Q	D	S	T	H	H
S	E	F	I	Q	U	A	P	S	G	O
E	J	F	O	S	P	O	O	N	S	N

Words Inside Words

Words often have other words inside them. For example, in the word "kitchen" we can find the words "it," "itch," "he," and "hen."

Find five or more words in the crossword that have other words inside them. Write the five words, and underline the "inside" words.

e.g., SPO<u>ON</u>S _____

_____

_____

_____

_____

5. Not odd; flat or smooth (4)
6. A large black-and-white animal which eats bamboo (5)
11. The hottest season of the year (6)
12. A dairy food made from milk (6)
13. A steep rock face usually near the sea (5)
16. We make these when we close our hands up tightly (5)
18. The sound of one's voice bouncing back from a hard surface (4)
19. The sister of one's father or mother (4)

Level A Unit 6
(Answers on page 56)

Find the Words

The ten down-words in the crossword are hidden in the square.

C	A	L	P	C	A	T	C	H	N	I
I	P	U	F	I	T	U	L	I	O	N
T	R	I	N	D	L	P	Y	G	O	T
A	N	S	G	R	A	P	E	S	S	O
B	Y	T	U	F	N	I	C	W	U	A
X	E	I	B	O	T	A	N	I	S	T
F	N	R	I	R	I	R	N	O	O	B
I	E	E	M	E	C	V	I	R	V	I
G	D	D	T	A	S	L	A	K	E	L
H	D	J	U	F	E	O	S	E	N	L
T	O	B	O	I	L	E	D	R	U	Y

Across

4. A cloud of vapor close to the ground (3)
7. Probable (6)
8. The past tense of "sing" (4)
10. Not guilty (8)
12. The low soft sound a dove makes (3)
15. To say something; Never – – – – a lie (4)
16. Usually a meal eaten in the late afternoon or evening time (6)
17. Wood floating in water (9)

Down

1. The jaws of a bird; statement of charges for food and drink (4)
2. A body of water surrounded by land (4)
3. The name of an ocean (8)
5. Fruit that comes in clusters (6)
6. To argue; physical hitting between two people (5)
9. One who studies plant life (8)
11. An egg can be fried or – – – – – –; water that has already been heated till bubbling (6)
12. To – – – – – a ball or a cold (5)
13. Drained of energy (5)
14. Enter; We came – – – – the classroom (4)

WORD LIST

ATLANTIC	COO	INTO
FOG	DINNER	LAKE
BILL	DRIFTWOOD	LIKELY
BOILED	FIGHT	SANG
BOTANIST	GRAPES	TELL
CATCH	INNOCENT	TIRED

Anagram

Find the word in the crossword that can be scrambled to make NO CENT IN.

_____

Level A Unit 7
(Answers on page 56)

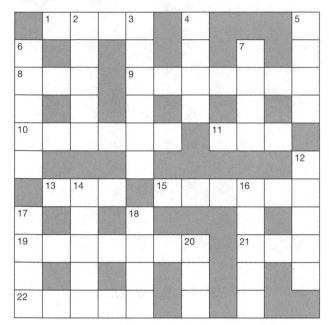

Find the Words

All of the <u>five-letter words</u> in the crossword are in this square.

P	R	O	X	T	R	O	P	S	W	E
L	I	G	I	M	E	S	U	H	I	F
P	S	U	N	Y	J	U	L	U	R	U
E	T	F	L	T	A	W	M	G	D	I
R	F	K	U	H	I	L	O	F	O	T
T	R	O	A	S	T	O	D	F	C	R
H	A	O	D	I	F	L	C	E	T	P
B	B	P	U	F	L	G	I	L	B	A
A	D	E	L	A	I	D	E	O	V	R
L	E	L	T	A	M	E	R	N	I	K
N	S	N	A	R	D	C	N	N	O	A

Across

1. A bird of prey (4)
8. A flightless Australian bird (3)
9. Roads with trees on either side (7)
10. A person who runs away from the law like Jesse James (6)
11. Another word for a eucalyptus tree (3)
13. Consumed food (3)
15. A disease caused by a vitamin C deficiency (6)
19. Word to describe tribal people who have no fixed dwellings and move from place to place (7)
21. This is left when wood has been completely burned (3)
22. A large hooded jacket worn in the Arctic (5)

Down

2. A fully-grown person (5)
3. Animals whose diet is eucalyptus leaves (6)
4. A plant may grow from this (4)
5. A bony fish; deep in tone (4)
6. A person who has committed a serious crime (5)
7. A personal religious teacher; an expert (4)
12. Traditional stories about the early history of a tribal group or country (5)
14. A person who trains circus lions is called a lion – – – – – (5)
16. Cook in an oven or over a fire (5)
17. Break with a sharp cracking sound (4)
18. A thought or suggestion about what could be done (4)
20. Abbreviation for Central Intelligence Agency (3)

Anagram

Find the word in the crossword that can be scrambled to make A TERM.

_____

Level A Unit 8
(Answers on page 56)

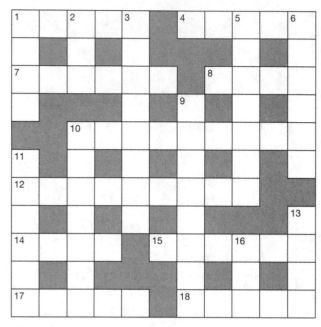

Across

1 In the shape of a cone (5)
4 The result at the end of the game (5)
7 Rectangular (6)
8 A male deer (4)
10 A period of two weeks (9)
12 The action of cutting something into two equal parts (9)
14 Employed; I – – – – a spoon to stir my tea (4)
15 A plane shape which is perfectly round (6)
17 More than is usual or expected (5)
18 A person who does this is either very tired or bored (5)

Find the Words

All ten of the underlined across-words in the crossword are hidden in this square, some running across and some running down. Can you find all of them?

Y	A	W	N	S	O	P	S	C	U	T
O	B	I	S	E	C	T	I	O	N	F
O	P	O	X	F	U	L	M	U	D	O
R	A	B	O	N	R	C	C	S	O	R
E	R	L	D	R	V	Y	B	E	H	T
D	I	O	S	C	O	R	E	D	V	N
E	V	N	G	O	M	P	R	A	N	I
X	N	G	S	N	P	R	S	T	A	G
T	I	C	L	I	I	D	O	E	G	H
R	S	B	C	C	I	R	C	L	E	T
A	S	W	Y	L	V	U	M	M	I	W

Down

1 The farmer harvests this after the growing season (4)
2 Nothing; no score (3)
3 A legal agreement (8)
5 A plane figure with eight sides and eight angles (7)
6 The product of 16 and 5 (6)
9 A number beyond any countable number; Buzz Lightyear says, "To – – – – – – – – and beyond!" (8)
10 Quickest (7)
11 An angle that is more than 90 degrees but less than 180 degrees (6)
13 Not as much; a smaller quantity (4)
16 Animal that gives milk (3)

Anagram

An anagram is the scrambling and rearranging of the letters of a word or words to make a new word or words. Rearrange the letters of the following words to make one word in the crossword.

BITE COINS _____

Name _____

Date _____

 **Unit 9**

(Answers on page 57)

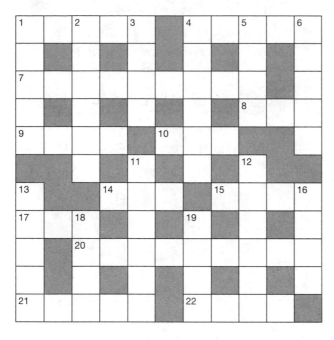

(Answers on page 57)

Find the Words

All the down-words in the crossword are in this square. Can you find all twelve of them?

A	S	P	R	O	N	A	L	L	O	W
F	C	R	E	W	I	M	I	N	T	P
T	A	U	N	P	T	E	R	M	U	L
U	R	S	L	I	N	D	K	L	X	X
R	E	T	V	U	G	A	N	D	E	R
C	D	P	R	N	L	L	A	B	N	E
L	I	N	B	O	U	G	H	F	E	X
O	H	G	Y	T	J	I	O	A	D	C
U	M	C	L	E	N	A	O	C	Y	E
D	R	X	P	S	M	I	S	T	T	P
S	U	O	F	L	R	P	R	U	L	T

Across

1. A magician performs this (5)
4. A punctuation mark which indicates a brief pause between parts of a sentence (5)
7. Likely to cause harm or injury (9)
8. The first prime number (3)
9. A vegetable related to an onion which may be used, with potatoes, in soup (4)
10. Not even (3)
14. Frozen water (3)
15. The plural of ox (4)
17. The opposite of on (3)
20. When people are happy to do the same thing, we say they have reached, or made, an – – – – – – – – – (9)
21. Disliked very much (5)
22. An important subject studied in school (5)

Down

1. Everyone who competes in the Olympic Games hopes to win this (5)
2. Male goose (6)
3. The sailors on a ship (4)
4. Masses of watery vapor floating in the atmosphere (6)
5. Clouds of tiny water droplets not as thick as fog (4)
6. Permit; let (5)
11. Afraid; frightened (6)
12. Not including; everyone was there – – – – – – John (6)
13. A main branch of a tree (5)
16. In music we should sing or play each of these correctly to create a tune (5)
18. Something which is known to be true (4)
19. One section of the school year in Australia (4)

Anagram

Find the word in the crossword that has the anagram ENTER GAME.

_____

Name _____

Date _____

Level A **Unit 10**
(Answers on page 57)

Insects

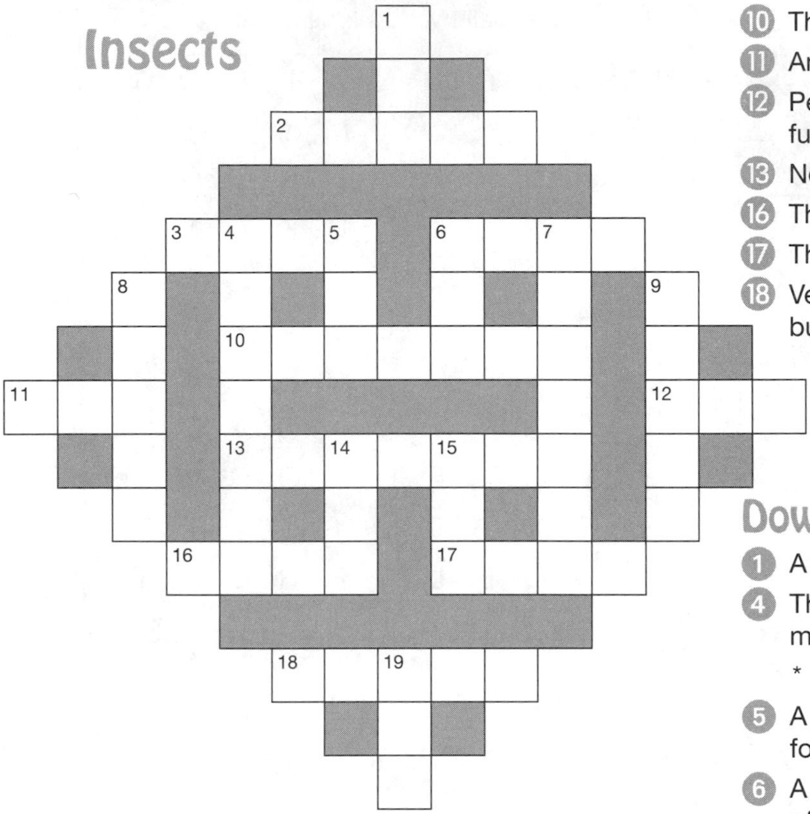

[crossword grid with numbered cells 1-19]

Across

2 Insects which fly towards lights at night (5)

3 These are not insects; they are small vipers (snakes) (4)

6 We must help to – – – – endangered species from extinction (4)

10 The main subjects of this crossword (7)

11 An insect which makes honey (3)

12 Pet animal which may have 8-down in its fur (3)

13 No longer living on this planet (7)

16 The largest continent (4)

17 This is on each wheel of a car (4)

18 Very annoying insects which buzz around food (5)

Down

1 A very busy little insect (3)

4 These are not insects; they are arachnids* and many of them make webs (7)

   * Pronounced [a-*rack*-nids]

5 A signal which may be sent by a ship calling for help (3)

6 A tiny bag, which contains poison, on the body of a bee (3)

7 A – – – – – – – to America may be frightened of 4-down (7)

8 Tiny hopping and biting insects found on pets (5)

9 Sometimes an insect bite makes us – – – – – , and we want to scratch (5)

14 A hot drink (3)

15 When we are camping, we may need this over our beds to keep the mosquitoes away (3)

19 This climbing plant which grows on walls may have lots of tiny 10-across on it (3)

Find the Words

All ten underlined across-words are hidden in the square. When you have found them, look for the insect (not in the crossword) which is hidden diagonally in the square.

B	E	E	B	S	T	U	R	T	I	P
G	U	L	T	D	C	N	I	I	Q	U
F	N	T	R	S	A	V	E	R	U	V
L	U	R	T	Y	T	E	I	E	L	P
A	D	A	F	E	X	T	I	N	C	T
R	U	S	N	P	R	L	N	T	U	K
F	I	P	Y	O	R	F	A	S	I	A
L	O	S	P	N	C	E	L	C	A	G
I	N	S	E	C	T	S	H	Y	K	L
E	T	N	O	K	U	I	W	N	L	J
S	U	J	K	N	F	M	O	T	H	S

Words from Words

How many words of three letters or more can you make with the letters of 4-down in the crossword? A score of five or more is good. _____

_____

_____

Name _____
Date _____

Level A **Unit 11**

(Answers on page 57)

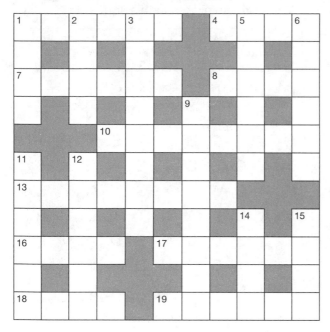

Find the Words

There are eight six-letter words in the crossword. All of them are hidden in this small square.

M	O	S	U	N	S	E	T	P
Y	B	K	I	E	A	O	M	M
C	R	O	W	D	S	V	R	I
A	A	M	U	L	H	E	D	S
U	N	I	F	G	O	N	X	L
G	C	P	O	S	S	U	M	A
U	H	G	N	B	C	E	R	N
S	L	U	K	H	I	J	L	D
T	E	F	A	S	T	E	N	U

Across

1. A summer month in America (6)
4. When the ocean tide flows away from the shore, we say it does this (4)
7. A marsupial that lives in trees that we might see at night (6)
8. Water from the sky (4)
10. On a family outing, we may cook our food on this (8)
13. In geography, we might say a town is 300 miles above this (3, 5)
16. Busy little insects (4)
17. A street, especially one with trees on either side (6)
18. A sand hill formed by the wind (4)
19. Lots of people in the same place (6)

Down

1. High mountains which may have snow on their peaks (4)
2. A sudden rush of wind (4)
3. Highly seasoned minced (ground) meat, usually pork, stuffed in casings (8)
5. A limb of a tree (6)
6. The name we give to the moment when the sun goes down (6)
9. Someone who watches what is happening (8)
11. Land which is completely surrounded by water (6)
12. Fix firmly so that it won't come undone (6)
14. In some countries this falls in the winter (4)
15. Oceans (4)

Anagram

Find the word in the crossword which has the anagram AS A GUESS.

_____

Unit 12

(Answers on page 57)

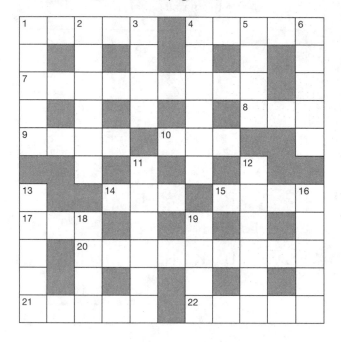

Find the Words

All the <u>down-words</u> in the crossword are hidden in this square.

S	T	E	A	P	O	E	T	L	T	O
E	R	A	S	T	B	E	L	L	O	W
Q	U	I	L	T	S	L	C	I	L	F
L	P	M	N	F	I	J	Q	N	O	M
O	V	I	Q	U	I	T	E	T	B	I
M	A	C	L	S	T	E	F	E	N	S
O	P	O	W	U	X	S	Y	N	Z	E
V	A	U	L	A	U	T	I	D	U	R
E	C	S	D	L	N	E	D	A	M	P
R	G	I	S	J	U	D	M	R	I	X
L	U	N	K	L	E	X	A	M	S	T

Across

1. Not noisy (5)
4. Repeat what someone else has said or written (5)
7. The part inside the lower body where digestion and other functions take place (9)
8. The edge of a cup (3)
9. An active volcano in Sicily (4)
10. A small swelling on the eyelid (3)
14. A child's plaything (3)
15. An organism that causes disease (4)
17. The fluid in a plant (3)
20. Things that stand in our way (9)
21. The language spoken in ancient Rome (5)
22. Strength; authority (5)

Down

1. Rather; this book is – – – – – interesting (5)
2. Have a plan; mean (to do something) (6)
3. A short examination (4)
4. Warm, padded bed covers (6)
5. Above (4)
6. Important big tests (5)

Words from Words

More than 50 words can be made from the letters of 20-across in the crossword.

Try to find at least eight words of four letters or more.

_____

_____

_____

_____

_____

11. My relative who is the child of my uncle or aunt (6)
12. The loud roar of a cow or a bull (6)
13. Normal; customary (5)
16. A person who hoards money and spends very little (5)
18. Writer of verse (4)
19. Slightly wet (4)

Name _____

Date _____

Level A — # Unit 13

(Answers on page 57)

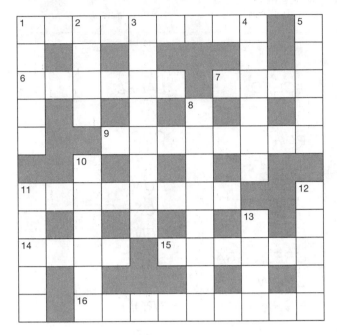

(Answers on page 57)

Find the Words

All the <u>five- and six-letter words</u> in the crossword are hidden in the square.

S	C	O	R	B	L	I	N	D	S	Y
F	A	L	U	X	O	R	T	I	N	D
E	N	O	I	B	C	L	F	L	T	N
V	A	R	N	I	S	C	Q	U	L	E
O	D	S	E	S	T	R	O	N	G	I
P	A	L	D	O	M	B	Q	U	G	G
M	Y	T	H	S	U	I	N	D	T	H
O	F	K	D	U	N	C	L	E	N	T
G	U	P	P	T	I	R	L	C	A	F
G	B	D	E	H	J	J	O	A	G	X
O	P	S	L	U	P	T	U	Y	W	X

Across

1. Become invisible; cease to exist (9)
6. The country to the north of the United States of America (6)
7. A present (4)
9. People who tell others how clever they (themselves) are (8)
11. Not probable; probably won't happen (8)
14. Sugar is grown in – – – – fields (4)
15. Powerful (6)
16. A very fast moving motorboat (9)

Down

1. Our teeth may do this if we don't brush them well (5)
2. Fine grains which cover most beaches (4)
3. Sometimes gates are locked with these (8)
4. Spoiled; damaged so badly that it cannot be repaired (6)
5. Traditional stories which often include supernatural beings (5)
8. Cut off from other people or places; lonely (8)
10. We close or pull these down in order to shut out the light (6)
11. My mother's or father's brother (5)
12. Ninety-six divided by twelve (5)
13. A ball game played on horseback (4)

Hidden Words

Two words from the crossword are hidden <u>backwards</u> in this sentence.

MOM SAID NASTY GIANTS THAT FIGURED IN FOLK TALES SCARED HER.

_____ _____

Name _____

Date _____

 **Level A** **Unit 14**
(Answers on page 57)

(Answers on page 57)

Here is a story crossword. The numbers, across or down, show where you should write the missing words in the crossword spaces. If you don't know a word, go on to the next one and come back to it later. It is best to put in the easy words first.

The Three Billy Goats

	1	2		3		4		5		6
7										
8				9						
10							11			
						12				13
	14	15			16			17		
18				19						
20								21		
22										

WORD LIST

ACHED	LABELS
BILLY GOATS	LATELY
BRIDGE	ODD
BROTHER	PREFER
DIETS	RUN
DRAG	RUNS OFF
EAT	SENSE
GREEN GRASS	SURE
GROW	TEETH
HORN	TROLL
IS NOT	USE

This is the story of three (1-across, two words) named Gruff. It has not rained (10-across). Their field is dry, and there is not much to (21-across). Their stomachs have often (5-down) from hunger, and all three look as if they are on (17-down)!

On the other side of a (16-across), they can see a beautiful field with lots of (22-across, two words), and they long to go to that field. But under the (16-across) lives a nasty old (7-down). He is very (11-across) and mean. He has put (3-down) all over the (16-across) warning animals that he will eat them if they try to cross it. But, at last, the biggest (9-across) says, "There (2-down, two words) enough grass to keep us alive, and we can't wait for more grass to (4-down). If we don't cross the (16-across), we will starve. We must (14-across) our brains to think of a plan."

They decide to trick the old (7-down). The littlest (9-across) bravely says, "I will go first!" He goes to the (16-across) and starts to walk across it, clip-clop, clip-clop.

Suddenly the old (7-down) calls from under the (16-across), "Who goes there?"

"It is I," says the littlest (9-across).

"I'm going to eat you!" shouts the (7-down).

But the littlest one says, "Oh, don't eat me; I have a big (9-across) who is very fat. I'm (6-down) you would (12-down) to eat him. He will be coming soon."

"Oh, very well," says the (7-down), "(8-across) along!," and the littlest (9-across) (20-across, two words) quickly to the beautiful field and starts to (21-across) the (22-across).

Then the second (9-across) comes along, clip-clop, clip-clop on to the bridge. He also persuades the old (7-down) to wait for the biggest (9-across). It is clear that the (7-down) does not have much (15-down)!

Then the biggest of the (1-across) comes along. Clip-clop, clip-clop go his hooves on the bridge.

"Now, I am coming up to eat you!" shouts the (7-down), jumping on to the (16-across), showing his sharp (13-down). But the biggest one is ready for him. He catches the old (7-down) on one big (19-down) and starts to (18-down) him to the edge of the (16-across). Suddenly the (7-down) leaps into the water and immediately turns into a stone. And the three (1-across) are probably still in the field enjoying the (22-across, two words) and growing bigger every day.

Find the Words

All the <u>verbs</u> in the crossword are hidden in this square. Remember that verbs are "doing words" (and sometimes "not-doing words").

```
E  A  T  D  R  O  N  W  A  V  L
R  I  M  R  Y  M  Y  H  R  M  R
U  K  I  A  C  H  E  D  P  V  U
E  T  B  G  K  U  R  E  R  O  N
D  I  S  N  O  T  C  R  E  D  S
P  F  T  B  O  M  L  T  F  S  O
R  L  O  N  G  R  O  W  E  I  F
E  O  P  O  S  L  I  N  R  P  F
U  S  E  W  G  R  J  O  L  C  Y
E  T  L  H  O  U  V  O  M  Y  U
R  K  B  I  L  N  O  Y  P  X  J
```

Anagram

Find the two <u>five-letter words</u> in the crossword which <u>both share</u> the anagram HE TESTED IT.

_____ _____

The Billy Goats' Story Continues

When the third Billy Goat joined his brothers in the nice green field, they were all very happy. They were enjoying the green grass when, suddenly, . . .

Now complete the story.

_____

_____

_____

_____

_____

_____

_____

_____

 Level B

Unit 15

(Answers on page 57)

Find the Words

In this smaller square seven words from the crossword are hidden.

L	E	V	K	O	F	N	I	W
I	D	E	R	T	E	R	K	S
R	K	N	I	D	N	I	S	H
G	I	F	T	I	K	F	Y	R
O	W	O	U	W	A	V	E	U
N	I	C	P	U	V	U	F	G
I	S	E	R	P	E	N	T	W
S	T	N	G	L	S	X	E	C
S	K	I	L	P	H	I	G	H

Across

1. Animals which have a diet of eucalyptus leaves (6)
3. Tall, flightless birds (4)
7. A big swell of seawater moving towards the shore (4)
8. We churn milk to make this product (6)
10. Another word for snake (7)
11. We can eat this boiled, poached, or fried (3)
12. We attach this to each shoe for gliding over snow (3)
13. Not for others to see (7)
15. Large enclosure in which birds are kept (6)
16. A present for someone (4)
17. The opposite of low (4)
18. Nearer (6)

Down

1. Flightless birds in New Zealand (5)
2. Informing the public of a new product that can be bought (11)
4. A subject which includes arithmetic, geometry, etc. (11)
5. Move the shoulders up and down, meaning "I don't know" or "I don't care" (5)
6. This is hung at the window for privacy (7)
9. A large spotted member of the cat family (7)
12. Violently break (5)
14. Come or go into (5)

Anagram

A. Find the word in the crossword which has the anagram RED OPAL.

_____

B. If you scramble all the letters of 10-across, you can make a 7-letter word which has the same meaning as 16-across.

_____

Level B Unit 16

(Answers on page 57)

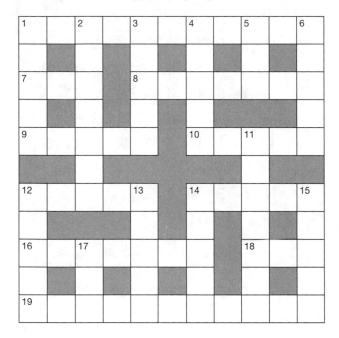

© Teacher Created Resources, Inc.

#8077 Vocabulary Puzzles & Activities

Find the Words

There are four <u>verbs</u> (doing words) in the down-words of the crossword. Can you find them in the square? (*Note:* 12-down is sometimes used as a verb but not in this crossword.)

S	T	R	G	N	I	R	U	P
T	R	E	F	L	I	A	B	L
O	I	R	O	U	C	K	I	E
G	H	E	L	P	S	E	L	X
L	U	P	S	L	U	D	K	E
S	F	L	I	Y	A	W	N	S
H	G	I	D	A	P	R	U	S
O	G	E	L	S	Q	U	N	E
V	U	D	K	T	U	F	G	R

Across

1. A boy who is a wizard and well-known in fiction and film (5, 6)
7. A part of the mouth (3)
8. Another word for wizard (7)
9. In or from Switzerland (5)
10. A meal eaten in summer (5)
12. A country in southern Asia (5)
14. Person who performs on the stage or in film or television (5)
16. Ancient Japanese soldier (7)
18. When I write, I – – – a pencil (3)
19. Machines used for writing letters before the invention of computers (11)

Down

1. Assists (5)
2. Gave an answer (7)
3. A person does this when tired or bored (5)
4. Ugly monsters, like giants (5)
5. A couple; a pair (3)
6. Used a garden tool to gather leaves (5)
11. Rabbits love to eat carrots and – – – – – – – (7)
12. A small illustration set in a bigger one (5)
13. An archer uses this with a bow (5)
14. A defense by an accused person that he/she was somewhere else at the time (5)
15. Ridges of rocks, often of coral, near the water's edge (5)
17. A picture of a part or the whole of the earth's surface (3)

Hidden Word

Find a word in the crossword by taking one letter from each word in the following sentence. (*Hint:* Selecting the letter in the same position in each word will <u>not</u> help.)

SAM SAYS COLIN ALWAYS SPEEDS.

_____

Anagram

Find the solution (answer) to one clue in the crossword which has the anagram TRY HERO TRAP. Guess and check!

_____

Name _____

Date _____

Unit 17

(Answers on page 58)

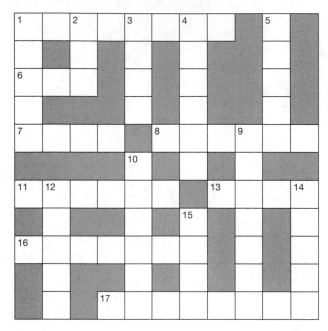

Find the Words

All the across-words are hidden in the square. Can you find all eight of them?

D	R	U	P	S	V	T	K	B	E	A
I	O	B	A	K	E	R	Y	U	O	R
F	L	I	S	O	J	L	L	D	E	R
F	M	F	O	J	U	A	R	G	W	E
C	L	O	T	H	E	S	X	E	G	S
L	I	R	I	N	X	F	Y	R	P	T
T	N	E	B	K	A	C	S	I	V	E
L	S	S	E	R	M	Y	T	G	I	D
E	X	T	F	U	P	R	T	A	C	U
A	M	R	U	S	P	I	D	R	X	T
P	R	T	O	R	T	O	I	S	E	M

Across

1. A slow-moving animal with a big shell (8)
6. A flower that has not yet fully matured (3)
7. An important school test (4)
8. Area with lots of trees (6)
11. The place where bread is made (6)
13. Jump high (4)
16. Things we wear to cover our bodies (7)
17. Taken by the police and accused of breaking the law (8)

Down

1. A piece of furniture in the dining room (5)
2. The color of blood (3)
3. Place where we bake food (4)
4. A member of the crew of a ship (6)
5. We use these with knives (5)
9. A high mountain first climbed by Edmund Hillary (7)
10. Person who uses a bow and arrow (6)
12. Let; permit (5)
14. Stood (or sat) in position to have my photograph taken (5)
15. Little island (4)

Backwards Fact

This fact has been written backwards. Rewrite it correctly on your own piece of paper.

DEIRD DNA, DENIARTS, TALF DEDNUOP, RETAW HTIW DEXIM EH HCIHW REBIF OOBMAB DNA KRAB YRREBLUM GNISU, NUL IA'ST, NAM ESENIHC A YB DETNEVNI YLBABORP SAW REPAP

Words Inside Words

Look at the words in the crossword, and see if you can find three words that have in them the same four-letter word meaning "stop working and relax."

_____ _____

_____ _____

 Level B

Unit 18

(Answers on page 58)

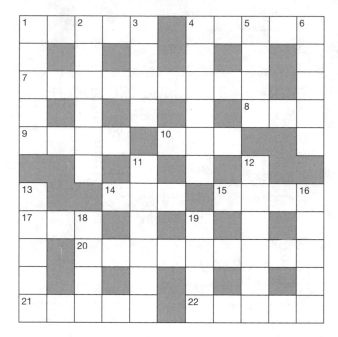

Find the Words

All the four-letter and five-letter down-words in the crossword are hidden in this square.

F	L	O	B	R	O	N	W	A	V	L
R	I	M	O	Y	M	Y	H	R	M	P
U	K	I	O	M	I	T	A	F	A	L
E	T	B	K	P	B	U	R	E	M	O
D	M	U	S	I	C	R	E	R	D	A
N	I	F	T	B	O	M	L	T	I	S
A	B	L	O	N	F	A	R	E	H	I
B	R	O	P	O	S	L	I	N	J	S
X	I	S	U	S	N	Q	U	J	O	L
C	Y	T	L	F	O	U	V	O	M	Y
V	E	K	B	I	L	D	O	Y	P	X

Across

1 This is struck to produce fire (5)
4 Not true (5)
7 Divides or keeps apart (9)
8 Also (3)
9 Cut with an axe (4)
10 Covered or soaked with liquid (3)
14 Honey-making insect (3)
15 A team game played on horseback (4)
17 The opposite of on (3)
20 Debates; disagreements with other people (9)
21 Perfume (5)
22 The Queen of Hearts is said to have made these (5)

Down

1 We make this when we sing or play an instrument (5)
2 Walk very quietly and carefully (6)
3 Animal like a large rabbit (4)
4 A male parent (6)
5 Misplaced or not able to be found (4)
6 Obtain pleasure from (5)
11 A word to describe how tall something is (6)
12 The place where two walls meet (6)
13 Printed matter that we enjoy reading (5)
16 Fertile place in the desert (5)
18 We must pay this when we travel on a bus or train (4)
19 Leave out (4)

Anagram

Find the word in the crossword which has the anagram EIGHTH.

_____

Name _____

Date _____

This is the well-known story of Goldilocks and the three bears. Can you fill in the blanks and put the words in the correct places in the crossword?

The Three Bears

WORD LIST

AGAIN	HUGE
AROMA	KNOB
BAD	MOTHER BEAR
BED	NIGHT
CANNOT	ORANGE
CAR	PORRIDGE
DANGER	POTATOES
EATEN	RUNS
EDGE	SAD
FAST	SNOOZE
FATHER BEAR	STOP

There is a little girl called Goldilocks who likes to walk in the woods rather than ride in a (11-down). One day she goes a little further than usual and finds herself looking at a nice little house. The house belongs to three bears, a (1-across: two words) and a (20-across: two words) and their little bear known as Baby Bear. The three bears have gone for a walk because (1-across) says that his (5-down) is too hot to eat. They have decided to walk right to the (18-across) of the woods.

Goldilocks goes up to the little house and knocks at the door. No one answers, so she knocks (2-down). Still there is no answer, so she slowly turns the round (17-down) and the door opens. Goldilocks is not afraid. She doesn't think she is in any (13-across). She doesn't (7-across) to think that she is doing something naughty, but runs straight into the bears' kitchen because she can smell a lovely (16-down) (another word for a nice smell). There she sees a table and chairs and three bowls of (5-down) on the table—a big bowl, a middle-sized bowl, and a tiny bowl. The big bowl is really very big because (1-across) is a (3-down) bear! Goldilocks decides to taste the (5-down). She tastes a bit from each of the bowls, but the only one which is just right is Baby Bear's. It tastes so nice that she can't (7-across) eating, and soon

she has (4-down) it all up. Goldilocks decides that (5-down) is her favorite food—much nicer than beans or (8-down). After she had finished the (5-down), she drinks a glass of the (6-across) juice which is on the table.

Then she goes to the living room where she finds three chairs of different sizes. The most comfortable chair is Baby Bear's very small chair. Unfortunately, she sits down too hard and breaks it! That is a very (12-across) thing to do.

Then she goes upstairs to the bedroom. She finds that the most comfortable (12-down) is the one belonging to Baby Bear, so she decides to lie down and have a quick (19-across) (another word for a short sleep).

While she is sleeping, the three bears come home and discover the (12-across) things that Goldilocks has done. Poor Baby Bear is very, very (9-down). When the bears come up to the bedroom, they find Goldilocks asleep. Goldilocks wakes up, jumps out of (12-down) and (10-across) as (15-across) as she can out of the house and doesn't (7-across) running until she is out of the woods.

The three bears (11-across) believe that a little girl could do such naughty things! Goldilocks decides that she will never (2-down) go near the woods, day or (14-down) and that she will never (2-down) go into another person's house without first being invited to do so.

Name _____

Date _____

Level B Unit 20

(Answers on page 58)

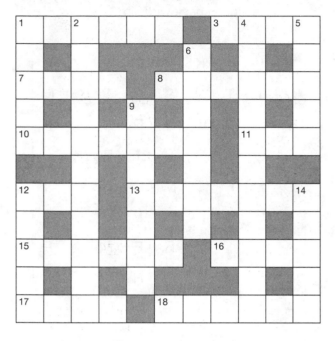

Across

1. One of the four seasons (6)
3. Not new; made use of (4)
7. Not wild or fierce (4)
8. Jumped about on one leg (6)
10. Comes back (7)
11. A sunbeam (3)
12. A form of public transport (3)
13. People who damage and destroy property (7)
15. Grown-ups (6)
16. Our bodies are covered with this (4)
17. Require; want very much (4)
18. Our food is usually put on these (6)

Down

1. Change (5)
2. Spaghetti sauce includes this ingredient (6, 5)
4. A very big grocery store where we may do the weekly shopping (11)
5. Another word for father (5)
6. Relatives who are the children of your aunt or uncle (7)
9. Not public; not for others to see (7)
12. The thinking part of our body (5)
14. Goes down towards the bottom of the water (5)

Anagram

Find the solution to a clue in the crossword that has the anagram CAT TO A MOUSE!

_____

Name _____

Date _____

Unit 21

(Answers on page 58)

¹		²		³		⁴		⁵		⁶
⁷									
						⁸			
⁹			¹⁰				
		¹¹					
¹²		¹³			¹⁴		¹⁵
¹⁶			¹⁷			
		¹⁸				
¹⁹			²⁰			

Across

1. We write on this (5)
4. We go to the dentist when our tooth does this (5)
7. A person who arrives after the lesson has started (9)
8. Tear up roughly (3)
9. One of the sections of the school year (4)
10. The twelve people in court who must decide whether someone is guilty (4)
13. Performs on the stage (4)
14. A place in which we swim (4)
16. Steal from (3)
18. These are put in the garden so that birds can wash themselves (9)
19. Insects which fly at night and are attracted to lights (5)
20. Areas behind houses (5)

Down

1. The driver of the airplane (5)
2. A naughty bunny who liked to go into Mr. McGregor's garden (5, 6)
3. Cliffs by the sea are made of this (4)

Find the Words

This is a difficult one. The first two across-words and the final two across-words (four words only) are hidden <u>backwards</u> in this square.

P	L	O	K	Y	T	B	K	L
U	I	T	N	S	H	T	O	M
V	M	H	I	V	R	C	R	E
S	O	R	S	L	I	R	K	L
D	E	F	E	M	D	A	J	J
R	V	O	H	B	L	V	O	Y
A	L	T	C	R	E	P	A	P
Y	M	U	A	O	R	R	X	L
A	I	N	X	T	M	U	S	I

4. A limb located on the upper body (3)
5. Famous wizard boy (5, 6)
6. We may walk up these to enter the school (5)
11. Begins (6)
12. This is used for sweeping (5)
15. Misplaces; no longer has (5)
17. Do what one is told to do (4)

Remove the Invader

An unwanted letter has invaded this piece of math information. Find the invading letter, delete it, and rewrite the sentence. (*Hint:* Don't delete the letter every time it occurs; sometimes it has a right to be there!)

TWTHOTLE TNUTMBERTS TARTE THTET COTUNTINTG NTUMTBERTST FROTMT TOTNET TOT TINFINTITY.

_____

_____

Level B Unit 22

(Answers on page 58)

1		2		3		4	5	6
					7			
8				9				
	10							
11								
12	13				14			
								15
16				17				
18			19					

Find the Words

There are eight <u>five-letter words</u> in the crossword. Seven of them are hidden in the square.

O	C	R	E	S	B	R	A	P	U	V
C	R	E	A	M	C	Y	T	O	L	T
B	I	N	W	A	J	I	T	S	V	N
T	O	V	E	N	S	P	I	D	E	D
S	T	I	L	N	I	L	C	U	O	M
I	T	L	M	U	N	E	H	G	U	B
F	E	P	K	A	B	E	V	E	N	T
G	R	I	S	L	W	R	K	E	I	F
K	L	U	N	T	L	S	L	S	S	L
E	Y	H	F	E	P	T	M	E	R	M
T	B	O	F	R	U	C	N	R	I	V

Across

1. A hot-tasting powder used for flavoring food (6)
4. Moist (4)
8. Change (5)
9. A fish-eating mammal of the weasel family which has a long body (5)
10. Persons who design buildings and supervise their construction (10)
12. Very popular sweets that can melt easily (10)
16. The fatty part of the milk used as a topping on apple pies (5)
17. Farmyard animals that make a honking sound (5)
18. A compass point (4)
19. A skillful public speaker (6)

Down

1. A Christmas song tells of a partridge in this fruit tree (4)
2. A boy's name (5)
3. Useful little creatures that live in the soil (10)
5. The room at the very top of the house, in or partly in the roof (5)
6. A small group of words which act as a unit in a sentence; a saying (6)
7. My shirt may be on this in the wardrobe (4, 6)
11. A hanging, tapered piece of frozen water (6)
13. Food is cooked in these (5)
14. A happening; one of the contests which make up a sports competition (5)
15. An animal with antlers (4)

Hidden Word

Three words in the crossword are hidden in this sentence:

ADAM, PAT, AND I MADE A STRONG HAMMOCK FROM ROPE—A REALLY GREAT ONE.

_____ _____ _____

Anagram

Find the word in the crossword which has the anagram HIT CARS, ETC.

_____

Name _____

Date _____

Find the Words

The four <u>eight-letter words</u> in the crossword are hidden in the square.

D	R	A	R	G	I	C	S	F	N	I
I	O	S	W	I	M	O	L	R	A	C
B	K	W	I	S	L	M	D	O	R	N
L	O	E	C	O	I	P	O	L	C	I
A	G	E	G	R	O	U	P	B	H	U
R	Y	P	L	N	A	T	Q	U	E	S
M	L	I	O	P	L	E	U	E	L	C
U	N	N	E	S	K	R	I	N	F	R
O	N	G	P	U	A	L	W	I	U	M
D	A	R	D	R	A	W	I	N	G	S
F	L	E	L	B	N	X	F	S	I	B

Across

1. Buildings or rooms containing collections of books (9)
6. Not awake (6)
7. We use this to stick materials together (4)
9. Pictures or diagrams made with pencil or crayon (8)
11. A useful device with a keyboard and a screen (8)
14. In grammar, the name for a person, place, or thing (4)
15. A class of fruits that include oranges and lemons (6)
16. Before we had e-mail, people used these to send urgent messages (9)

Down

1. Gain knowledge (5)
2. We hear this when the school day is about to start or end (4)
3. You and your classmates belong to the same – – – – – – – – (3, 5)
4. Making no sound (6)
5. A board game in which you checkmate your opponent's king (5)
8. Keeping the floor clean with a broom (8)
10. Quantity (6)
11. Shapes with circular bases; ice cream comes in these (5)
12. We may sit at these to do our homework (5)
13. The amount of space a flat surface takes up (4)

Which Words

Some of the words in the crossword are concerned with communication and information. Can you name four?

_____ _____ _____ _____

Name _____

Date _____

 Level B **Unit 24**
(Answers on page 58)

	1	2		3		4		5		6
7										
8				9						
10						11				
					12			13		
	14	15		16			17			
18			19							
20						21				
22										

Across

1. At school we study science and – – – – – – – – – – (10)
8. Owing (3)
9. The name of one highly industrialized country which has a president as its leader (7)
10. All the money and property a person owns (6)
11. Number of years since birth (3)
14. People do this on stage in the theater or in films (3)
16. Strength and vitality (6)
20. A female sheep (3)
21. An insect that can sting (3)
22. The amounts to be paid regularly to meet a debt (10)

Down

2. Choose someone for a position by voting (5)
3. Soundness of body; freedom from disease (6)
4. Not closed (4)
5. Due for payment (5)
6. A period of twelve months (4)

Find the Words

All the words in the crossword which start with a vowel are in the square.

A	C	T	E	L	O	N	T	A	G	E
E	K	W	U	A	W	Y	X	Q	U	I
W	R	U	K	L	I	B	O	P	E	N
E	F	A	L	N	N	R	L	L	A	N
C	R	D	E	B	G	O	C	O	M	C
T	I	D	L	E	D	U	C	P	E	F
O	V	E	M	L	O	N	D	I	R	I
R	K	D	U	E	E	T	W	O	I	S
P	O	G	B	C	V	R	A	J	C	D
E	S	T	A	T	E	U	B	J	A	U
S	M	U	L	E	N	E	R	G	Y	V

7. I – – – – – the numbers to make a total (5)
12. False (6)
13. My computer has 512 mega – – – – – of memory (5)
15. Not expensive (5)
17. A machine that can be programmed to carry out complicated tasks automatically (5)
18. An animal with antlers (4)
19. Remain (4)

Which Word?

It is possible to make a story about one of the across-words in the crossword if you separate its parts slightly. The <u>outside</u> letters of the word give us what the landlord expects to receive. <u>Inside</u> is a demand by the landlord! On the lines below write first what the landlord expects to receive and then write the landlord's demand.

_____   _____

Level B Unit 25
(Answers on page 59)

(Answers on page 59)

Find the Words

In this smaller square, twelve words from the crossword are hidden.

C	R	S	E	W	S	T	R	C
B	R	O	T	H	E	R	E	U
Y	S	C	R	U	B	B	L	B
E	I	S	F	A	M	I	L	Y
T	W	T	L	S	L	F	U	S
I	F	A	B	L	E	F	D	U
S	S	G	L	B	J	L	A	N
I	K	S	E	F	O	R	D	I
P	I	C	E	N	S	U	S	T

Across

1. Parents and their children; a group closely related (6)
3. Fathers (4)
7. One and the other; the two together (4)
8. A girl sibling (6)
10. A line of hair just above an eye (7)
11. A young member of a bear family (3)
12. Some families like to go to the snow and do this in the winter (3)
13. A day of the week (7)
15. Not awake (6)
16. A single item; a home – – – – (4)
17. Uses a needle and thread (4)
18. Every ten years, when this is taken, we must give information about the people in our household (6)

Down

1. An old story, often about animals (5)
2. The relationship of Dad's mother to Mom (6-2-3)
4. A word meaning one's ancestors and family background (11)
5. Rub very hard with a brush to make something clean (5)
6. Halfway through the week (7)
9. A boy sibling (7)
12. Adult male deer (plural) (5)
14. Large, furry man-like creatures believed to inhabit the snows of Tibet (5)

Words in Words

Find three words of three letters or more in the right order inside 4-down.

_____ _____

_____ _____

Level B ## Unit 26
(Answers on page 59)

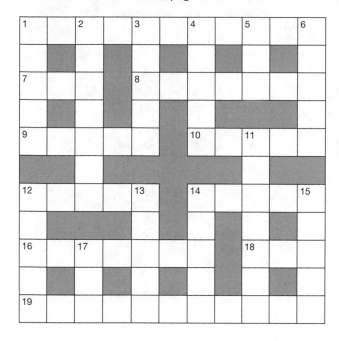

Find the Words

Find four words from the crossword which might be used in a geography lesson.

S	T	R	E	E	M	S	K	O
A	R	F	I	D	L	E	X	U
F	O	M	P	L	G	H	I	C
G	L	I	N	D	I	A	N	G
I	L	O	B	E	R	E	S	X
O	V	A	L	L	E	Y	S	T
B	R	S	M	T	U	L	P	T
E	M	I	P	A	Q	U	E	N
L	I	S	U	R	G	Y	I	W

Across

1 Belonging to a time long ago; before recorded history (11)

7 This remains when wood or other material has been burned (3)

8 Periods of ten years (7)

9 The triangular area of sediment that may be at the mouth of a river (5)

10 Clothing worn by women in India (5)

12 Does not eat any food for a set period (5)

14 The course of a spacecraft around a star or planet (5)

16 Low areas between hills or mountains (7)

18 Mom – – – the candles on my birthday cake (3)

19 A reptile that makes a warning sound with its tail (11)

Down

1 Fabric woven with colored yarn in a cross-barred pattern, sometimes used to make a skirt (5)

2 Breathes out (7)

3 A country in Asia (5)

4 Short, sharp-pointed nails used in carpentry (5)

5 A bright color (3)

6 A new computer – – – – – quite a lot of money (5)

11 Another name for German measles (7)

12 A body temperature that is higher than normal (5)

13 A silvery-gray metal (5)

14 A fertile spot in a desert (5)

15 The name of a person, film, or book, etc. (5)

17 Allow (3)

Anagram

Find the word in the crossword which has the anagram NEAT TALKERS.

_____

Name _____

Date _____

Level B **Unit 27**
(Answers on page 59)

Communicating

1		2		3		4		5	
6									
7				8			9		
			10						
11	12					13		14	
					15				
16									
		17							

(Answers on page 59)

Find the Words

All the words in the crossword which start with the letter A are in the square.

F	L	A	S	P	R	C	N	A	D	S
S	O	M	T	U	R	A	D	M	I	T
I	A	B	L	T	I	G	W	K	L	F
H	N	O	U	A	N	S	W	E	R	K
S	T	R	I	N	D	P	I	A	N	T
F	O	L	Y	T	W	U	G	B	I	R
E	N	R	I	E	T	B	C	U	R	N
S	Y	M	I	N	T	B	C	U	R	N
D	M	L	F	N	W	R	U	D	P	A
I	N	S	T	A	C	T	E	D	D	Y
O	U	N	D	S	P	L	E	U	S	N

Across

1 Radio and television aerials (8)

6 These sets communicate information and entertainment in words and pictures (11)

7 A cartoonist communicated an idea when he – – – – a cartoon (4)

8 A comment (6)

11 Morse code is a means of communicating using dots and what else? (6)

13 This sign communicates the order that we must go no further (4)

16 Native Americans used to communicate by lighting a fire and sending this kind of signal (5, 6)

17 Broadcast or send out a radio or television signal (8)

Down

1 A mime actor communicated when he – – – – – but didn't speak (5)

2 Speakers; those who communicate with spoken words (7)

3 Ships of this branch of the defense forces communicate with flags, flashing lights, and radio (4)

4 Reply (6)

5 A person who gives money to support an organization (5)

9 A word which is opposite in meaning to another word (7)

10 Another word for a shooting star (6)

12 Agree that something is true or confess that you have done something wrong (5)

14 The person who flies the plane (5)

15 Some people who cannot hear well speak to each other in – – – – language (4)

Anagram

Which word in the crossword has the anagram, I SENT OLIVES?

_____

Level B **Unit 28**
(Answers on page 59)

Find the Words

All the <u>four-letter and five-letter</u> <u>down-words</u> in the crossword are hidden in this square.

P	A	P	I	R	I	N	S	O	F	K
R	A	I	F	C	A	I	R	O	S	T
U	N	I	K	Q	U	E	S	F	O	N
P	A	T	H	S	T	R	I	C	H	M
L	W	U	R	L	N	E	S	T	F	U
B	C	U	S	T	Y	M	B	E	R	M
R	D	E	P	F	R	K	S	P	O	M
O	G	M	E	H	I	J	P	L	S	Y
O	P	P	N	R	A	R	E	T	L	Y
F	M	U	D	N	E	S	E	G	S	T
O	P	L	I	D	P	R	D	E	G	T

Across

1 Bend over (5)
4 Our jeans may be made of this material (5)
7 The people who live in the country of the pyramids (9)
8 A boy's name; a male cat (3)
9 A song for two voices or two instruments (4)
10 A small collapsible bed often used when camping (3)
14 A family pet or a lion (3)
15 The family of animals that includes gorillas and chimpanzees (4)
17 The invisible gas that surrounds the earth (3)
20 Say "I am sorry" for something I have done (9)
21 A very large sea (5)
22 Mended; repaired (5)

Down

1 The rate at which a vehicle moves (5)
2 We cannot live without this important gas which our lungs take in (6)
3 A trail laid out for walking (4)
4 A mythical monster (6)
5 Home for a baby bird (4)
6 A body buried in ancient Egypt, preserved by wrapping (5)
11 A large ground-dwelling monkey (6)
12 An ancient stone figure in Egypt which has the body of a lion (6)
13 The capital city of Egypt (5)
16 Use money or time (5)
18 Not often seen (4)
19 The top part of a house or other building (4)

Anagram

Find the word in the crossword which has the anagram TINY PAGES.

_____

Remove the Intruder

Remove the letters which do not belong in this sentence, and then write the sentence. (*Note:* The first word has a letter "C.")

CCHCICMPCACNCZECECS CANCD CBCABCOCOCNCS BCELOCNCG TCOC CDCIFCFCERCENT FACMCICLICECS.

_____

_____

Name _____

Date _____

 Level B **Unit 29**
(Answers on page 59)

(Answers on page 59)

Find the Words

All the <u>across-words</u> are hidden in this square.

```
S O T E M A G N E T P
F R W I E N F L A T Y
C T I L B C D G H O L
P R S U G L A F R O K
Y O T A L S O O P I I
E F S B L O N H U R N
A T R A P E Z O I D S
R O G C F R I G P L T
B C D U Q Y E A H N E
L E G S T R U Y F B P
X N U M B E R L I N E
```

Across

1 These quadrilaterals have two parallel sides and two sides which are not parallel (10)

6 A calculator made of wires and beads (6)

7 A word a person shouts when his or her team is winning (4)

10 Too; as well as (4)

11 Winds around; curls and bends (6)

12 Also (3)

13 The curve under one's foot (6)

15 Level; not sloping (4)

18 Twelve months make one (4)

19 A piece of metal that attracts smaller metal objects to it (6)

20 A marked line used for practice in adding and subtracting (6, 4)

Down

2 Large quantities of printing paper, each about 500 sheets (5)

3 The sign for addition (4)

4 Frozen water (3)

5 The maximum quantity that a jug or other container can hold (8)

8 Pause because I am undecided on what to do or say next (8)

9 A factor of 8 and 12 (3)

11 The highest point (3)

12 The product of 2 and 5 (3)

14 A large or dense group of flying insects such as bees (5)

16 A cloth woven from flax; some tablecloths are made of this (5)

17 Of more than average height (4)

Anagram

Which word in the crossword has the anagram SHE ATE IT ?

_____

My Story

Choose five words in the crossword, and write a short story using those words. Underline your chosen words.

_____

_____

_____

_____

_____

_____

_____

_____

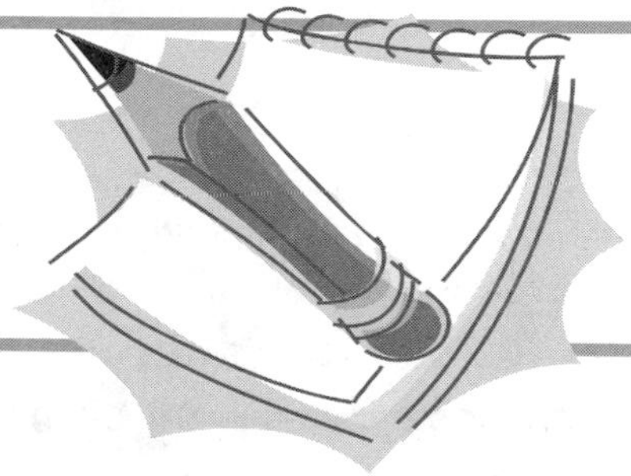

Words in Words

Some of the words in the crossword have another word in them. Write the words with the following meaning and the words from which they come. An example: "To be in debt" is "owe" (from "showers").

A Everything _____ _____

B Had something to eat _____ _____

C Something for the head _____ _____

D A major town _____ _____

E We hear with this _____ _____

F This keeps the mosquitoes out _____ _____

G Without feeling _____ _____

H Occupy a chair _____ _____

I We set this to catch an animal _____ _____

J Nice and cozy _____ _____

Name _____

Date _____

Unit 30
(Answers on page 59)

Find the Words

All of the six-letter words in the crossword are hidden <u>diagonally</u> in the square.

A	C	R	I	P	U	L	D	T	U	A
F	L	U	A	X	N	T	S	B	C	D
L	M	N	D	V	T	P	X	Y	Z	P
Q	U	F	R	I	I	D	N	T	Y	R
U	P	S	T	L	F	A	L	O	X	N
H	O	U	U	T	C	F	R	U	N	Y
P	O	T	D	L	S	H	P	Y	K	J
J	O	R	H	H	I	N	E	T	V	X
P	U	R	S	T	R	O	G	R	I	G
O	V	E	X	E	B	C	I	L	R	M
T	R	U	B	L	S	F	U	M	P	Y

Across

1. A large enclosure where birds are kept (6)
3. Grasp very firmly (4)
7. These become flowers when they open (4)
8. Bright cup-shaped flowers, often yellow (6)
10. The class of animals to which snakes and lizards belong (7)
11. Your cat is hungry; have you – – – him? (3)
12. Lair for a wild animal (3)
13. Another name for a eucalyptus tree (3, 4)
15. A small, dark red fruit with a pit (6)
16. Equipment that is easy to manage is said to be – – – – friendly (4)
17. When the gelatin does this, it is ready to eat (4)
18. Animals that we can ride (6)

Down

1. A dark orange-yellow color (5)
2. Free from other people's authority; self-governing (11)
4. Dense wet forests in tropical areas (4, 7)
5. Sat for my photograph or portrait (5)
6. We may see the skeletons of prehistoric animals in these buildings (7)
9. These are on our hands (7)
12. Farm birds that "quack" (5)
14. My brother – – – – – money by doing odd jobs (5)

Anagram

Which <u>two</u> words in the crossword, mixed together, give the anagram DEFEND?

_____ _____

Name _____

Date _____

 Level B ## Unit 31
(Answers on page 59)

Find the Words

All the <u>five-letter words</u> in the crossword are hidden in this square.

S	T	R	O	B	B	L	U	K	S	Y
H	F	R	U	E	R	T	L	C	M	V
O	U	D	R	E	A	L	T	E	R	I
O	R	D	E	R	V	P	R	U	T	W
T	R	U	B	R	E	K	Q	U	E	N
A	O	F	I	B	C	D	U	Q	U	N
S	T	I	P	L	E	R	R	J	O	P
T	H	R	E	E	G	R	U	G	B	Y
E	E	F	D	P	G	Y	R	C	D	F
X	E	X	U	V	M	N	A	R	P	S
B	E	C	T	M	O	N	L	I	F	F

Across

1. Any animal that walks on two feet (5)
4. Change in some way (5)
7. Greek philosopher who was the tutor of Alexander the Great (9)
8. One of the bones in the chest (3)
9. Female sheep—plural (4)
10. To decorate with; – – – – the Christmas tree (4)
13. Mom – – – – a computer to write letters (4)
14. Do not include; leave out (4)
16. A male sheep (3)
18. The word for paper or plastic money (9)
19. Belonging to the countryside, not the town (5)
20. The square root of nine (5)

Down

1. Courageous (5)
2. The word for any number which has two factors only, itself and one (5, 6)
3. Obligation; it is your – – – – to come to school on time (4)
4. One of the major blood vessels in the body (6)
5. This is used for measuring body temperature (11)
6. A well-known ball game that was started in England; a game very similar to football (5)
11. What a piece of corn is called before it is popped (6)
12. Instruction or command (5)
15. The one of the five senses which concerns the tongue (5)
17. We make this when we tie two pieces of string together firmly (4)

Hidden Words

Three words from the crossword are hidden in these sentences:

WE VISITED AN ART GALLERY IN THE WEST AND LEARNED A LOT FROM IT. WE BROUGHT BACK NOTICES ABOUT THE NEXT EXHIBITION.

_____ _____

_____

Level B — Unit 32
(Answers on page 59)

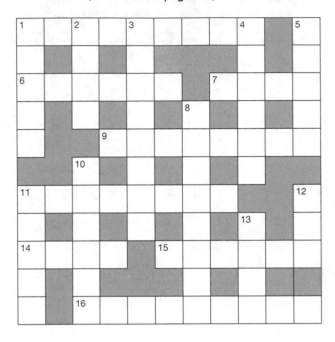

Find the Words

The four <u>eight-letter words</u> in the crossword are hidden in the square.

P	L	A	C	N	T	U	R	F	U	L
R	M	E	M	E	N	T	O	S	T	E
S	T	R	I	G	A	B	C	U	R	F
D	E	F	G	R	I	L	I	N	G	S
E	N	O	N	A	G	O	N	S	O	R
D	E	K	I	L	O	G	R	A	M	Y
P	Q	U	T	W	V	S	U	R	K	X
E	L	I	I	G	R	Y	F	U	R	G
B	O	L	N	H	I	J	O	P	S	T
V	A	N	G	L	U	S	D	R	U	P
A	B	U	C	R	F	R	E	G	L	D

Across

1. Plane figures consisting of three straight sides and three angles (9)
6. One-sixtieth of a minute (6)
7. A vehicle for hire (4)
9. Setting fire to; lighting (8)
11. Objects kept as souvenirs or reminders (8)
14. Close to (4)
15. Curved structures forming a part of some bridges (6)
16. A distance of 1,000 meters (9)

Down

1. Short class examinations (5)
2. The unit of measure, used before decimal currency, equal to 2.54 cm (4)
3. Plane figures consisting of nine sides and nine angles (8)
4. The crackly noise sometimes made by a radio; nonmoving (6)
5. (An amount) not yet paid (5)
8. A unit of mass equal to 1,000 grams (8)
10. Go on board a ship or plane (6)
11. The sign which means "take away" in subtraction (5)
12. The past form of "is" (3)
13. Closed; not open (4)

Which Words?

List the six words in the crossword which are concerned with measurement or shape.

_____ _____ _____ _____

_____ _____

Name _____

Date _____

 Level B # Unit 33
(Answers on page 60)

All the five-letter words in the crossword are hidden in this square.

M	A	S	M	U	L	O	S	I	F	P
U	K	S	U	P	U	O	I	P	L	E
S	U	O	N	E	O	M	D	R	U	B
I	N	C	D	S	D	S	E	A	T	S
C	A	K	U	T	P	P	S	H	L	O
H	D	S	T	A	F	F	U	B	O	N
I	E	P	L	Y	L	I	G	R	O	C
G	S	O	L	R	K	Y	A	C	U	H
L	K	H	T	I	C	K	S	P	L	I
E	S	J	O	F	I	L	X	I	Z	N
D	P	Y	F	L	S	T	A	L	D	A

Across

1 Each year we celebrate these as we get older (9)
8 The opposite of "No" (3)
9 Fancy dress; we may wear this in a school performance (7)
10 These keep our feet warm (5)
11 We sit on these (5)
13 We make this with instruments and with our voices (5)
15 A rectangle has four of these (5)
17 The name by which the United States is also known (7)
19 Put food into the mouth and swallow (3)
20 A morning meal (9)

Down

2 Very small creatures (7)
3 Dogs and cats get fleas and – – – – – (5)
4 We may sit at these in the classroom (5)
5 The word we use when addressing another person (3)
6 The organs of sight (4)
7 We sleep in these at night (4)
12 The house, street, and city where you live (7)
13 Breakfast, lunch, or dinner (4)
14 Pandas live in this country in Asia (5)
15 A word which includes all the teachers at a school (5)
16 Is seated (4)
18 One of the two organs of hearing (3)

Words from Words

How many three-letter words can you make from the letters in 12-down?

_____

_____

_____

Anagram

Find the word in the crossword which has the anagram CUT SOME.

_____

Name _____

Date _____

Level B — Unit 34
(Answers on page 60)

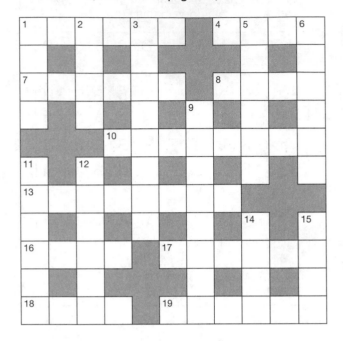

Find the Words

All the <u>across-words</u> are hidden in the square.

S	A	B	U	R	G	L	A	R	S	H
C	L	U	P	O	I	E	F	A	P	E
R	T	I	W	I	F	R	E	O	I	D
F	I	F	L	O	T	P	A	G	L	O
I	M	U	S	E	U	M	T	T	D	V
O	B	M	U	S	N	P	H	W	I	A
B	E	B	L	T	A	C	E	O	B	L
T	R	E	B	T	U	K	R	O	U	K
Y	T	H	U	M	B	S	S	C	L	O
G	A	T	E	L	U	I	V	K	E	O
R	Q	U	S	V	A	G	R	E	E	D

Across

1. Collections of dinosaur bones may be seen in this place (6)
4. A large edible fish often sold in a can (4)
7. On our hands we have two of these (6)
8. A present (4)
10. Birds have these (8)
13. People who steal from houses (8)
16. Egg-shaped (4)
17. Wood used in house building and carpentry (6)
18. A movable barrier in a fence (4)
19. Consented; said, "Yes" (6)

Down

1. A fable about nature, the world, and the people in it (4)
2. Closed (4)
3. This keeps us dry when it rains (8)
5. Joined; combined; the – – – – – – Nations is an association of countries (6)
6. Someone who paints or draws pictures (6)
9. Beginning (8)
11. Rectangular figure (6)
12. A pupil who stays away from school without permission (6)
14. A woodwind musical instrument (4)
15. Stepped; walked (4)

Words from Words

More than sixty words of <u>three letters or more</u> can be made from the letters in the word FEATHERS. How many can you make? You may use a word in the singular or in the plural, but not both (e.g., if you choose "fee," you must not also use "fees"). And only one form of the verb is accepted (e.g., if you use "hate" you may not also use "hates"). A score of fifteen or more is very good. Use your own paper if you need more space.

_____
_____
_____
_____
_____
_____

Level B Unit 35
(Answers on page 60)

©Teacher Created Resources, Inc.

Find the Words

All of the <u>five-letter words</u> in the crossword are in this square.

D	L	I	D	E	R	N	O	S
S	T	A	T	E	L	U	R	B
I	D	E	I	I	P	L	D	A
G	E	O	G	R	O	G	E	S
V	K	V	E	A	B	C	R	I
F	O	E	R	E	I	G	N	C
D	A	A	N	S	G	E	R	N
F	L	N	P	D	R	I	V	E
D	A	X	U	S	E	G	N	G

Across

1. A place where ships load and unload cargo (4)
6. An animal in the cat family that is striped with black (5)
8. A unit of a nation having a federal government; Arizona is an example (5)
9. Works produced from a creative person (3)
10. The opposite of wild (4)
12. To give assistance (4)
16. Long poles with blades at the end to help steer a boat (4)
18. Fries are made out of this vegetable (6)
21. The opposite of inside (7)
22. To operate a vehicle such as a car (5)
23. Moved from one place to the other (11)

Down

2. Moving from one boundary to the other; She traveled – – – – – – – the forest (7)
3. Too; likewise (4)
4. An animal whose diet is eucalyptus leaves (5)
5. Followed a command (6)
6. One who interprets another language (10)
7. An opening in a wall or fence (4)
11. Another word for sick (3)
13. A person who you see when you are sick (6)
14. Belonging to a place by birth; – – – – – – American (6)
15. A small sheltered inlet or bay (4)
17. The time or – – – – – of a king or queen (5)
19. A command that is given (5)
20. Another word for cry (4)

Anagram

Find the word in the crossword that can be scrambled to make TO A POT.

_____

#8077 Vocabulary Puzzles & Activities

Level B # Unit 36
(Answers on page 60)

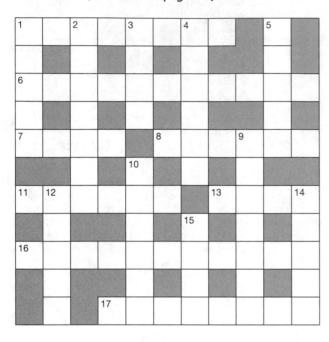

Find the Words

All the four-letter and five-letter words in the crossword are in the square. Can you find them?

S	P	I	G	E	F	M	I	O	V	U
C	A	N	A	L	I	I	D	S	A	B
R	E	F	R	D	O	O	R	S	G	S
U	G	I	F	R	B	N	O	H	S	T
P	R	K	L	I	U	C	G	Q	U	I
S	T	M	E	A	R	S	U	U	J	R
I	A	P	A	G	M	M	L	O	V	A
B	R	O	G	E	O	I	P	H	W	I
A	S	F	U	D	F	L	O	N	N	B
L	O	I	K	U	L	E	L	P	X	I
U	N	L	E	K	T	L	C	U	R	E

Across

1 A shortage of supply; insufficient quantity (8)

6 Something which holds our attention or curiosity is very – – – – – – – – – – (11)

7 These are on both sides of your head (4)

8 Kind; not rough (6)

11 A person who cannot stop using a drug or other substance (6)

13 A small, hopping, biting insect that can be found on cats and dogs (4)

16 Those who take part in a competition or a dispute (11)

17 To put in jail (8)

Down

1 A facial expression showing pleasure, friendliness, or amusement (5)

2 Changed (7)

3 Remedy; get rid of a disease by treatment (4)

4 Ate a small portion to test the flavor (6)

5 A man-made waterway (5)

9 Natural skills or abilities (7)

10 A loud, piercing cry (6)

12 Barriers in houses which can be opened and closed (5)

14 The criminal act of setting fire to property intentionally (5)

15 Move very slightly; mix liquid ingredients (4)

Words from Words

The solution to 1-across in the crossword is not a very big word, but more than forty words of three letters or more can be found in it. How many can you find? A score of ten or more is good.

_____
_____
_____
_____
_____
_____
_____

Name _____

Date _____

Level B Unit 37
(Answers on page 60)

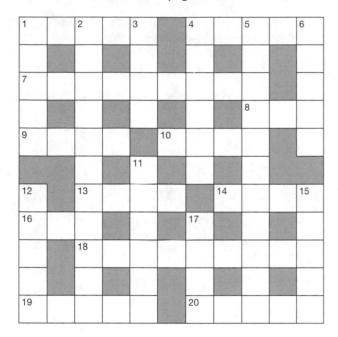

There are twenty-two words in the crossword. <u>Ten of them</u> are in this square.

F	R	A	L	L	I	G	A	T	O	R
I	C	O	F	A	C	T	S	H	G	U
L	O	M	I	N	S	H	F	R	R	D
T	N	F	A	T	H	E	R	A	E	S
E	D	O	K	N	O	I	D	V	W	T
L	U	D	A	H	U	R	L	S	O	R
M	C	I	C	O	M	Y	B	L	M	U
O	T	R	L	I	T	W	E	L	V	E
V	O	T	I	R	H	X	C	A	Z	L
U	R	Y	S	E	L	M	I	J	U	M
G	H	P	H	V	O	N	F	I	F	S

Across

1. We must eat – – – – – and vegetables every day (5)
4. The one before the sixth (5)
7. The director of the orchestra, band, or choir (9)
8. Long snake-like fish (3)
9. It is worn on the foot (4)
10. It is usually green, and it grows on a plant (4)
13. Puts seed in the soil (4)
14. Old (4)
16. Belonging to him (3)
18. A large, fierce reptile found in America (9)
19. This is made in poetry when two words have the same sound (5)
20. Before the usual or expected time (5)

Down

1. Things and happenings we know to be true (5)
2. Not needed; not required to be done (11)
3. Not false; real (4)
4. We probably call him "Dad" (6)
5. One of the brave people who help to put out the flames (11)
6. Throws with great force (5)
11. The number of months in a year (6)
12. Word meaning "belonging to them" (5)
15. Grubby; not clean (5)
17. An ugly monster in legends and fairy tales (4)

Which Word?

Remove the first letter from one of the crossword answers to find a word that means "one who inherits." Write both words below.

_____ _____

Anagram

Find the word in the crossword which has the anagram GORILLA AT.

_____

Name _____

Date _____

Level B Unit 38
(Answers on page 60)

(Answers on page 60)

1		2		3		4		5		6
7										
							8			
9				10						
				11				12		
13		14				15				16
17		18				19				
		20								
21						22				

Find the Words

All the three-letter and four-letter words in the crossword are in this square.

H	I	G	H	W	I	S	L	E
I	G	H	2	O	M	Y	N	B
L	N	I	D	R	S	E	H	Y
A	S	H	C	J	I	R	I	T
P	O	S	E	A	S	A	B	E
U	T	U	P	Q	U	S	P	A
R	U	G	S	K	I	I	T	T
R	N	M	L	A	O	L	I	R
K	A	S	U	H	O	E	G	X

Across

1. These occur when the seas rise and fall on the shore under the influence of the moon (5)
5. A tool used for gardening (3)
7. An Italian word for beautiful (5)
8. The chemical symbol for water (3)
9. Long periods of history (4)
10. The residue that is left behind when something is burned (3)
14. Mineral spring with special water believed to improve health (3)
15. A large fish; we can buy it in a can (4)
17. Some do this on snow, and some do it on water (3)
20. Places where big seagoing vessels are built and repaired (9)
21. The hard, protective outer case of an oyster (5)
22. A country through which the Nile River flows (5)

Down

1. The level under the ground where the earth is saturated with water is called "the water − − − − − " (5)
2. These are triangular-shaped areas of sediment at the mouths of some rivers (6)
3. Large bodies of salt water (4)
4. A word for "smells" (usually bad) which may come from standing water (5)
5. Sometimes the tide is low, and sometimes it is − − − − (4)
6. A word (a part of the human body) often used to describe a bend in a river (5)
11. Rivers never flow in this direction (6)
12. The sound a cat makes when it is contented (4)
13. We are all water − − − − −, but we must not waste it. (5)
16. A useful or valuable thing (5)
18. This word is sometimes used in poetry to describe a small area of land surrounded by water (4)
19. A unit of computer information (4)

Anagram

Find the word in the crossword which has the anagram HIS DRY SAP.

_____

Name _____

Date _____

Level C **Unit 39**
(Answers on page 60)

Antarctica

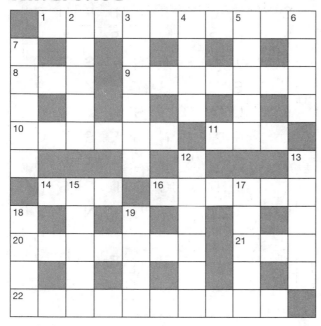

The author of this article is Nick Lovibond, Information Services, Australian Antarctic Division.

To the south of Australia, across the vast Southern (2-down) is a great continent called (22-across). Seabirds like the (18-down) and albatross (19-down) the (2-down), often following ships. The wandering albatross has the longest wingspan of any seabird in the world—a (10-across) of 3.8 yards or 3.5 meters tip to tip. As you approach (22-across), you might (14-across) an Emperor (9-across). You may even see chicks waiting to be (11-across).

Tens of millions of years ago, (22-across) was much further north, a warm continent with (12-down) similar to lands we know today. As (22-across) moved south, the (21-across) isolated it from other continents, and the area developed a cold and dry climate. As snow fell, it compacted, and built up as (8-across) covering the land, in some places up to 2.5 miles or 4 kilometers thick. Glaciologists get a (20-across) glimpse into past climate by drilling deep in this (8-across). Tiny bubbles of air, trapped in the snow when it fell hundreds of thousands of years ago, give us a (17-down) standard of clean pure air. This is an (13-down) record for scientists who are measuring changes in our atmosphere.

The land mass of (22-across) has (7-down) and valleys, and the tops of the tallest mountains poke up through the (8-across)-cap, a bit like some

Find the Words

The six <u>five-letter words</u> in thecrossword are hidden in the square.

F	L	O	D	E	R	N	T	S
R	I	N	T	K	L	U	M	B
I	D	E	H	I	L	L	S	A
G	E	O	P	R	O	G	L	S
V	A	C	T	A	B	C	X	I
F	L	E	G	Y	P	T	I	C
D	R	A	N	S	G	O	R	N
F	I	N	P	L	O	L	E	R
D	A	B	U	S	E	I	N	G

pyramids that stick up from the sands of (15-down). In winter months the surface of the sea around (22-across) freezes too, like a giant skating (4-down).

The environment in (22-across) is very fragile, and we must not (5-down) it. Though there are research stations and (3-down) of fuel and food left for emergencies, international rules insist that we (6-down) leave any trash. They also (16-across) disturbing any wildlife. This amazing (1-across) remains a continent devoted to science and peace.

WORD LIST

ABUSE	FOREST	RINK
ANTARCTICA	HILLS	SEA
BASIC	ICE	SEE
DEPOTS	IDEAL	SKUA
DON'T	KEYHOLE	SOAR
EGYPT	LENGTH	WONDERLAND
FED	OCEAN	
FORBID	PENGUIN	

Anagram

Which word in the Word List has the anagram

AN END WORLD ?_____

Level C **Unit 40**
(Answers on page 60)

Find the Words

All the words in the crossword which start with the letters P or S are hidden in this square.

S	P	E	C	O	P	A	L	P	U	R
T	R	A	S	G	U	K	S	L	U	P
S	P	I	D	F	P	R	I	S	T	O
I	A	S	P	A	S	T	A	K	S	P
F	R	U	Y	O	S	S	P	I	N	C
L	I	G	R	E	N	G	E	S	T	O
A	S	N	A	K	E	L	A	X	B	R
S	H	I	M	B	C	D	R	O	S	N
E	S	T	I	G	L	E	S	N	O	P
M	U	R	D	I	R	S	F	L	U	G
I	N	T	I	S	P	R	E	G	M	Y

Across

1. Cease to be visible; cease to exist (9)
8. Small green vegetable that grows, with others, in a pod (3)
9. A solid shape with a base and three or more triangular sides (7)
10. Loud, unpleasant sound (5)
11. A reptile (5)
13. Macaroni, spaghetti, etc. (5)
15. Birds which are symbols of peace (5)
17. Kernels of corn, heated until they burst, then eaten as a snack (7)
19. The upper or outer edge of a cup or a wheel (3)
20. Large, powerful seabird which can fly long distances (9)

Down

2. Sloping print in books and newspapers (7)
3. Enough or more than enough; plentiful (5)
4. The capital city of France (5)
5. One limb of the body (3)
6. Turn round very fast (4)
7. Not working; having nothing to do (4)
12. In grammar, parts of speech which tell how, why, when, or where something happened or was done (7)
13. Young dogs (4)
14. A Hawaiian word of greeting (5)
15. A person who donates something, such as money or blood (5)
16. A word prefix meaning "half," as in – – – – circle (4)
18. A friend (3)

Break the Code

In this sentence, the wrong vowels have been used in every word. Write the sentence correctly on the line.

ONYUNA WHA CIN RAID THES DASORVUS O SPACOUL TRAUT.

_____

Name _____

Date _____

Unit 41

(Answers on page 61)

Food, fabulous food

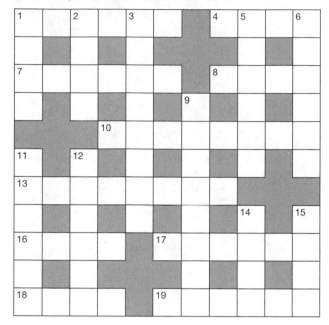

Across

1. Instructions for the preparation of a dish (6)
4. Covered with icing; made cold, perhaps in the freezer (4)
7. A large, yellow, melon-like fruit; papaya (6)
8. A medicine; a habit-forming substance which can harm the body (4)
10. Spring onions (8)
13. Let food stand in a specially-prepared liquid for some time before it is cooked (8)
16. We like our lettuce to be crisp, not – – – – (4)
17. Eggs are usually sold in – – – – – – (6)
18. We may do this to a salad to mix the ingredients well (4)
19. Very sweet, thick liquids added to sweet dishes or used to preserve fruits (6)

Down

1. Mature and ready to be eaten (4)
2. These animals give us milk (4)
3. A method of cooking eggs or fish by simmering in a small amount of liquid (8)
5. An orange-colored root vegetable (6)

Find the Words

All the <u>across-words</u> are hidden in the square.

L	I	S	D	E	N	S	U	F	L	E
I	I	R	K	D	O	Z	E	N	S	Y
M	U	N	F	L	I	G	N	K	S	M
P	P	S	H	A	L	L	O	T	S	A
R	A	F	L	E	N	B	O	C	X	R
O	W	I	G	N	D	R	U	G	F	I
S	P	L	U	N	T	E	L	P	Y	N
E	A	T	O	S	S	C	R	I	M	A
S	W	A	E	R	N	I	C	E	D	T
O	E	G	H	J	U	P	O	Q	U	E
S	Y	R	U	P	S	E	L	V	G	E

6. This is what our stomach and intestines do with the food we eat (6)
9. Eating too much; one of the "seven deadly sins" (8)
11. This is made of beaten eggs and cooked in a frying pan (6)*

   *There is another way to spell this word.
12. Pleasant smells which may come from the kitchen (6)
14. A list of dishes available in a restaurant (4)
15. Mom – – – – three eggs to make this cake (4)

Words from Words

About 20 words of <u>four letters or more</u> can be made from 3-down in the crossword. A score of eight is good.

_____ _____

_____ _____

_____ _____

_____ _____

_____ _____

Name _____

Date _____

Level C Unit 42
(Answers on page 61)

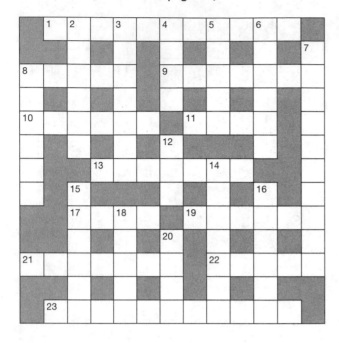

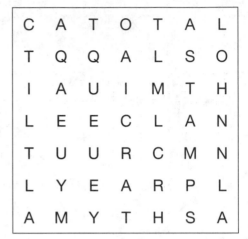

Find the Words

All the <u>four-letter and five-letter words</u> in the crossword are hidden in this small square.

C	A	T	O	T	A	L
T	Q	Q	A	L	S	O
I	A	U	I	M	T	H
L	E	E	C	L	A	N
T	U	U	R	C	M	N
L	Y	E	A	R	P	L
A	M	Y	T	H	S	A

Across

1. A contest between individuals or teams (11)
8. A line of people or vehicles waiting for attention or to move forward (5)
9. A structure made of pieces of wood or other material interwoven in a criss-cross pattern (7)
10. This covers the eye when it is closed (6)
11. A group of interrelated families; a word commonly used in Scotland (4)
13. A curved structure forming a passage or entrance (7)
17. Too; as well as (4)
19. Pour through a sieve to separate liquid from solids (6)
21. Tell a story of events; provide a commentary to accompany a film (7)
22. Traditional stories about early history often involving strange beings (5)
23. The boy who is my stepfather's son is my – – – – – – – – – – – (11)

Down

2. Did what one was told to do (6)
3. The first in position, rank, or importance; first time (7)
4. Tip to one side (4)
5. The result when figures are added together (5)
6. Vegetables which can make us cry when we cut them (6)
7. Advises that certain action should be taken (10)
8. Not kings, but – – – – – – (6)
12. This may be the first word of a question (3)
14. Try (7)
15. A bird that can imitate the human voice (6)
16. A fight between armed forces (6)
18. Put the foot down heavily; something we put on an envelope (5)
20. A period of twelve months (4)

Anagram

Find the word in the crossword which has the anagram NOTICE, I'M TOP !

_____

Name _____

Date _____

Level C **Unit 43**

(Answers on page 61)

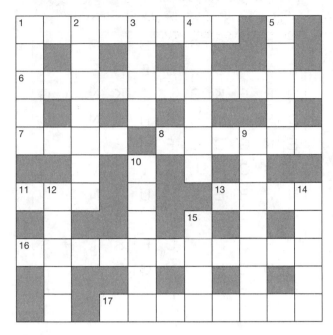

Across

1. One way to increase a number (8)
6. Another word for sharp angles (5, 6)
7. Every time we take a – – – – forward we are nearer to our destination (4)
8. A prime number has only two factors, – – – – – – and 1 (6)
11. The past tense of "light"; she – – – the candles (3)
13. When I had to multiply two big numbers, I – – – – my calculator (4)
16. The action of finding the length, or other dimensions, of something (11)
17. People who study (8)

Down

1. Most people eat three of these each day (5)
2. In comparing volume of sound, the opposite of quietest (7)
3. A thought that comes into one's mind (4)
4. We measure this in inches, feet, etc. (6)
5. One of our five senses (5)
9. The opposite of western (7)

Find the Words

All the words in the crossword which start with a vowel are hidden backwards in the square.

S	A	P	D	E	A	E	D	I	G	N
P	L	A	L	D	F	E	R	D	N	N
R	E	S	M	E	T	I	O	N	I	T
N	R	I	B	S	Q	U	F	E	L	D
R	I	K	S	U	M	O	L	T	E	D
E	B	I	C	K	I	F	E	C	I	B
T	L	K	E	L	S	U	S	O	U	N
S	E	L	G	N	A	E	T	U	C	A
A	X	E	R	P	T	L	I	B	I	M
E	I	F	P	I	R	L	C	R	O	D
M	D	G	I	R	N	L	U	A	H	G

Words in Words

Words with the following meanings are found <u>inside</u> words in the crossword, with their letters in the correct order. Write each word and the crossword word in which it appears.

A. Had something to eat
   _____ _____

B. Sever, using a knife, saw, etc.
   _____ _____

C. A cave in which a wild animal may rest
   _____ _____

D. In folk tales, a small person with pointed ears _____ _____

E. Very strict and serious
   _____ _____

F. A word meaning "certain"
   _____ _____

G. A small amount given to a waiter as appreciation for service
   _____ _____

10. Another word for "answer" in a mathematical calculation (6)
12. The articles or things on a list (5)
14. The days, months, and years in which events occurred (5)
15. A very heavy metal (4)

Name _____

Date _____

Level C Unit 44
(Answers on page 61)

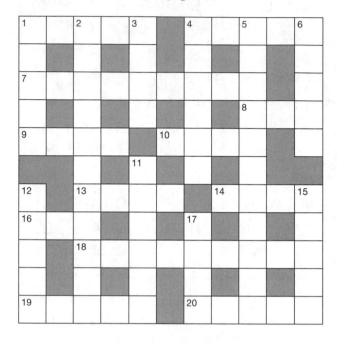

Find the Words

There are 22 words in the crossword. Ten of them are in this square.

T	R	U	O	B	L	B	L	O	F	Y
E	S	H	O	E	S	E	R	S	E	N
G	R	E	K	B	L	I	K	N	A	G
D	R	E	M	U	S	R	I	N	S	D
E	N	G	O	G	F	U	F	B	T	C
S	S	C	H	L	O	T	E	M	T	H
N	P	R	E	E	B	U	R	N	S	W
O	F	E	R	H	I	J	N	K	O	A
W	R	S	H	R	U	B	S	T	H	S
I	G	E	F	Y	V	O	Q	U	R	P
S	P	R	A	E	D	S	M	I	R	S

Across

1. Plants with leafy fronds in gardens and national parks, especially in rainforests (5)
4. Destroys or harms by fire (5)
7. Agreeing, or confessing, that something is true (9)
8. A long-handled gardening tool (3)
9. Not dangerous; domesticated (4)
10. Fine particles which we wipe from furniture (4)
13. Large, flightless Australian birds (4)
14. This falls from the sky in white flakes (4)
16. She is reading – – – own book (3)
18. A triangle with two equal sides and two equal angles (9)
19. A brass instrument, like a small trumpet, used in the army (5)
20. Garden flowers which usually have thorns (5)

Down

1. A big meal, usually celebrating a special occasion (5)
2. An antonym of "forgetting" (11)
3. Place where a building is located or where an event took place (4)
4. The capital city of Lebanon (6)
5. Angles of ninety degrees (5,6)
6. These are worn on the feet (5)
11. The continent of which Italy and Greece are a part (6)
12. A plant that is smaller than a tree (5)
15. Stinging insects (5)
17. A mark on the skin left by a healed wound (4)

Anagrams

Make an anagram for each of the following words in the crossword:

9-across   10-across   3-down   17-down

_____   _____   _____   _____

Level C **Unit 45**
(Answers on page 61)

Animals

1		2		3		4		5		6
7										
							8			
9				10						
			11				12			
13		14				15				16
17		18				19				
		20								
21						22				

Find the Words

All the <u>five-letter words</u> in the crossword are hidden in the square.

S	M	O	T	H	S	E	R	S	U	B
O	D	L	U	D	N	E	L	P	D	U
F	S	U	S	I	K	O	A	L	A	N
A	K	S	K	Q	U	I	B	M	U	N
W	S	I	S	F	O	B	C	R	U	M
N	U	L	P	A	Y	E	R	S	R	Y
S	E	H	I	C	J	O	L	A	S	I
P	R	I	S	T	K	L	O	M	P	B
S	W	I	M	S	T	P	O	B	E	L
I	X	Y	B	O	C	E	D	L	Y	N
M	P	E	L	T	I	W	C	E	E	N

Across

1. Things known to be correct and true (5)
4. Monkeys and chimpanzees are included in this family (3)
7. Australian marsupials smaller than kangaroos (9)
8. A male cat is sometimes called this; the boy's name is – – – (3)
9. In cold or wet weather, farm animals may shelter in this (4)
10. The foot of certain animals (3)
14. A honey-making insect (3)
15. An animal with backward-curving horns and, sometimes, a beard (4)
17. A nocturnal bird (3)
20. Echidnas are also known as "splny – – – – – – – – –" (9)
21. Walk at a leisurely pace (5)
22. Insects which fly at night (5)

Down

1. Young deer (plural) (5)
2. Young cows (6)
3. A fish-eating aquatic mammal with flippers (4)
4. Any living thing which is not a plant (6)
5. The direction which is opposite to west (4)
6. A fish does this (5)
11. An insect with wings which are hard on top (6)
12. A mammal such as a rat or a mouse (6)
13. Australian animal whose diet is eucalyptus leaves (5)
16. Elephants and walruses have these big teeth (5)
18. One young sheep (4)
19. The place where we might find cows, sheep, geese, or growing crops (4)

Name _____

Date _____

Level C — Unit 46
(Answers on page 61)

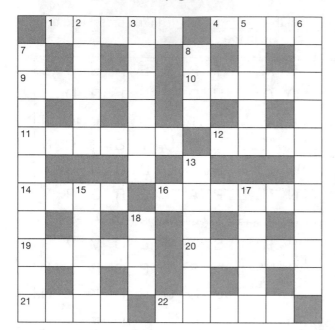

All the <u>five-letter words</u> in the crossword are hidden in this square.

S	P	E	A	D	D	E	D	N	N	G
F	I	H	S	D	R	I	N	I	N	K
A	G	L	W	O	E	L	M	G	I	E
G	L	U	P	S	N	F	R	H	R	E
B	O	C	T	O	D	A	Y	T	A	C
H	O	J	L	O	E	I	G	H	T	H
A	D	O	O	N	D	P	F	T	Y	E
T	U	E	N	P	W	R	U	G	Y	S
L	I	G	I	P	S	I	G	Q	U	S
A	O	N	D	Z	B	C	E	H		
S	O	J	N	R	M	E	T	U	W	Y

Across

1. Finished (5)
4. A very long poem, story, or film about the deeds of heroes (4)
9. A factor of 104 and 24 (5)
10. An edible bulb (5)
11. Fully grown, its growing period ended (6)
12. The sound of this tells us that recess has finished (4)
14. Tidy (4)
16. Those who have won every heat or match will compete in the – – – – – – (6)
19. After the night has ended, tomorrow will become – – – – – (5)
20. Home for an Inuit (5)
21. The longest – – – – of a right triangle is the hypotenuse (4)
22. This game ends in checkmate (5)

Down

2. When day has ended, this follows (5)
3. Complete; whole (6)
5. At the end of the game, the winner might receive this (5)
6. The end of something; the summing-up (10)
7. This is the end of the journey; the bus or train – – – – – – – – – here (10)
8. At the end of the performance, the audience claps and the performer should do this (3)
13. End; conclude (6)
15. When I have – – – – – all the numbers, I write the total below (5)
17. A book of maps (5)
18. The final three letters of the alphabet (3)

Check the Anagram

The first <u>two</u> letters of all the across-words added together and mixed up will give us this anagram: OHO! BIG FINE MINCE PIES EATEN! Check to see if this is correct.

_____

_____

_____

_____

Create-Your-Own Wordsearch

Directions: Choose your own words, and write them at the bottom. Then, insert the letters of the words into the word search boxes (one letter per box). Fill them in horizontally, vertically, or backwards. Fill in the empty boxes with random letters. Then, have a friend find the answers.

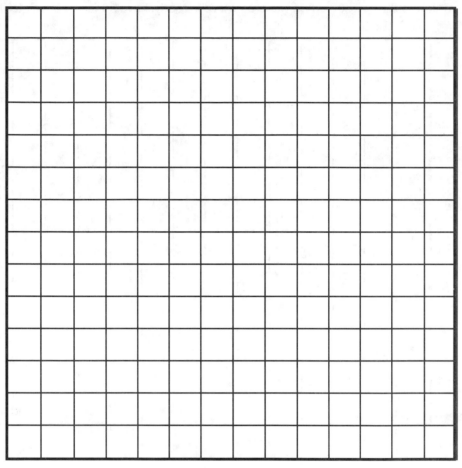

Word List

_____   _____   _____

_____   _____   _____

_____   _____   _____

_____   _____   _____

_____   _____   _____

_____   _____   _____

_____   _____   _____

🔲🔲Create-Your-Own Crossword🔲🔲

Directions: Choose your own word list at the bottom. Then, figure out where to put the words on the grid (only down or across). Make sure to label with the appropriate numbers. Then, darken all the unused boxes. Make sure all answers fit. Write your clues for the words on page 55, and make sure the numbers (Ex. 1-down) match to the puzzle. When the crossword is ready, have a friend complete the puzzle.

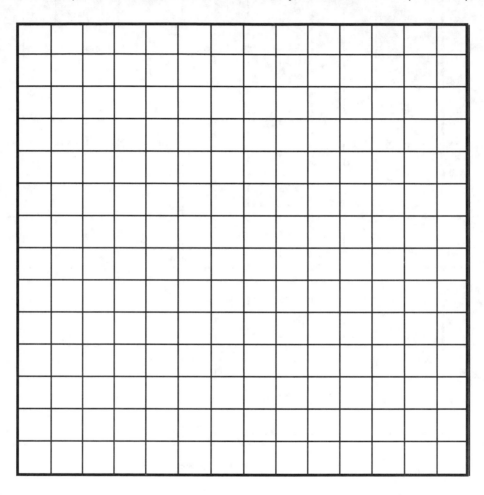

Word List

_____   _____   _____

_____   _____   _____

_____   _____   _____

_____   _____   _____

_____   _____   _____

_____   _____   _____

Create-Your-Own Clues

See page 54 for directions.

Across

_____ _____
_____ _____
_____ _____
_____ _____
_____ _____
_____ _____
_____ _____
_____ _____
_____ _____
_____ _____
_____ _____

Down

_____ _____
_____ _____
_____ _____
_____ _____
_____ _____
_____ _____
_____ _____
_____ _____
_____ _____
_____ _____
_____ _____

Level A – Answers

Unit 1   Page 5

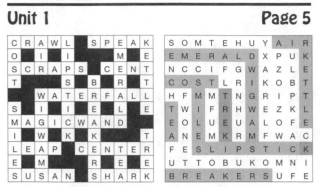

Anagram: 10-across, WATERFALL

Unit 2   Page 6

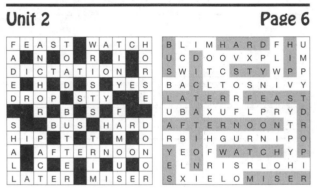

Anagram: 7-across, DICTATION

Unit 3   Page 7

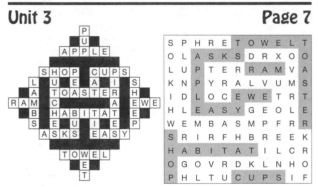

Anagram: 10-across, TOASTER

Unit 4   Page 8

Anagram: 10-across, PELICANS
Words from Words: ORANGE—age, are, ear, earn, ego, gear, gore, nag, near, nor, oar, ogre, one, rag, rage, ran

Unit 5   Page 9

Words Inside Words: For discussion

Unit 6   Page 10

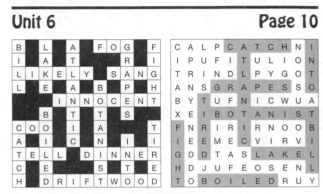

Anagram: 10-across, INNOCENT

Unit 7   Page 11

Anagram: 14-down, TAMER

Unit 8   Page 12

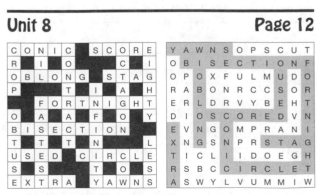

Anagram: 12-across, BISECTION

Levels A & B – Answers

Unit 9   Page 13

Anagram: 20-across, AGREEMENT

Unit 10   Page 14

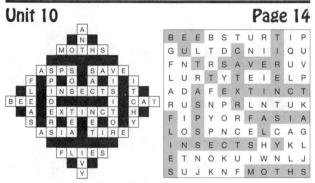

Words from Words: SPIDERS—dies, dips, dress, dries, drips, pie, press, pride, red, ride, rip, ripe, rise, sides, sips, sir, *and more*

Unit 11   Page 15

Anagram: 3-down, SAUSAGES

Unit 12   Page 16

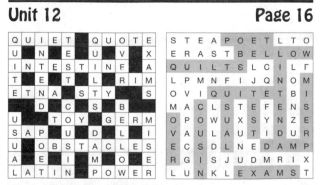

Words from Words: OBSTACLES—able, acts, also, base, bats, beast, belt, best, boat, cable, case, castle, class, cost, east, eats, last, less, lets, lost, sale, salt, oases, oats, scales, seat, seas, sets, steal, table, tale, toes, toss, *and many more*

Unit 13   Page 17

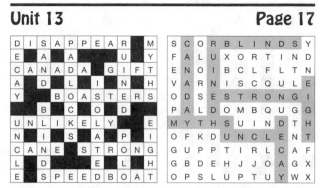

Hidden Words: [*backwards*] 2-down, SAND (SAID <u>NAS</u>TY);
7-across, GIFT (THA<u>T FIGURED</u>)

Unit 14   Pages 18–19

Anagram: 13-down, TEETH and 17-down, DIETS

Unit 15   Page 20

Anagrams: **A** 9-down, LEOPARD; **B** SERPENT – PRESENT = GIFT

Unit 16   Page 21

Anagram: 1-across, HARRY POTTER
Hidden Word: 10-across, SALAD (the first letter of the first word, the second letter of the next word, and so on)

Level B – Answers

Unit 17　　　　　　　　　　　　　Page 22

Words Inside Words: REST, in ARRESTED, EVEREST, AND FOREST
Backwards Fact: PAPER WAS PROBABLY INVENTED BY A CHINESE MAN, TS'AI LUN, USING MULBERRY BARK AND BAMBOO FIBER WHICH HE MIXED WITH WATER, POUNDED FLAT, STRAINED, AND DRIED.

Unit 18　　　　　　　　　　　　　Page 23

Anagram: 11-down, HEIGHT

Unit 19　　　　　　　　　　　　　Page 24

Anagram: (none)

Unit 20　　　　　　　　　　　　　Page 25

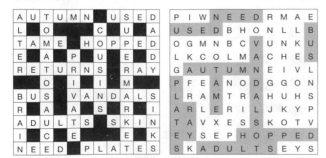

Anagram: 2-down, TOMATO SAUCE

Unit 21　　　　　　　　　　　　　Page 26

Remove the Invader: WHOLE NUMBERS ARE THE COUNTING NUMBERS FROM ONE TO INFINITY.

Unit 22　　　　　　　　　　　　　Page 27

Hidden Words: 4-across, DAMP (A<u>DAM, PA</u>T); 18-across, EAST (M<u>ADE A ST</u>RONG); 1-down, PEAR (R<u>OPE, A RE</u>ALLY)
Anagram: 10-across, ARCHITECTS

Unit 23　　　　　　　　　　　　　Page 28

Which Words?: 11-across, COMPUTER; 9-across, DRAWINGS; 1-down, LEARN; 1-across, LIBRARIES; 14-across, NOUN; 16-across, TELEGRAMS

Unit 24　　　　　　　　　　　　　Page 29

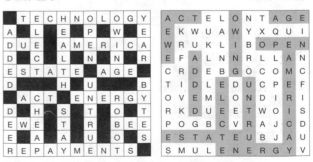

Which Word?: RE[PAYME]NTS — RENTS, PAY ME

Level B – Answers

Unit 25 — Page 30

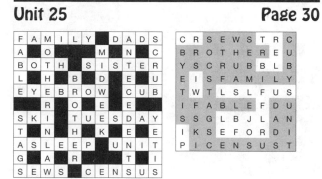

Words in Words: ant, cede, den, dent(s)

Unit 26 — Page 31

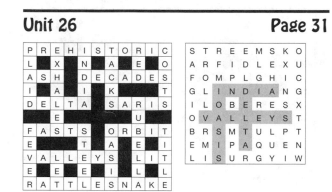

Anagram: 19-across, RATTLESNAKE

Unit 27 — Page 32

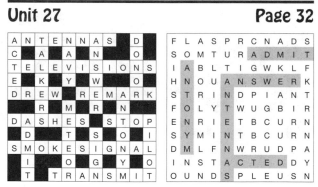

Anagram: 6-across, TELEVISIONS

Unit 28 — Page 33

Anagram: 7-across, EGYPTIANS
Remove the Intruder: CHIMPANZEES AND BABOONS BELONG TO DIFFERENT FAMILIES.

Unit 29 — Pages 34–35

Anagram: 8-down, HESITATE
Words in Words: **A** ALL (17-d. tall) **B** ATE (8-d. hesitate)
C CAP (5-d. capacity) **D** CITY (5-d. capacity) **E** EAR (18-ac. year) **F** NET (19-ac. magnet) **G** NUMB (20-ac. number line) **H** SIT (8-d. hesitate) **I** TRAP (1-ac. trapezoids) **J** WARM (14-d. swarm)

Unit 30 — Page 36

Anagram: 11-across, FED and 12-across, DEN

Unit 31 — Page 37

Hidden Words: 9-across, EWES (THE WEST); 14-across, OMIT (FROM IT); 17-down, KNOT (BACK NOTICES)

Unit 32 — Page 38

Which Words?: 15-across, arches; 2-down, inch; 8-down, kilogram; 16-across, kilometer; 3-down, nonagons; 1-across, triangles

Levels B & C – Answers

Unit 33   Page 39

Words from Words: ADDRESS—add, are, dad, ear, era, red, sad, sea   *Anagram:* 9-across, COSTUME

Unit 37   Page 43

Which Word?: 12-down, THEIR - HEIR
Anagram: 18-across, ALLIGATOR

Unit 34   Page 40

Words from Words: Answers will vary because many words can be made.

Unit 38   Page 44

Anagram: 20-across, SHIPYARDS

Unit 35   Page 41

Anagram: 18-across, POTATO

Unit 39   Page 45

Anagram: 1-across, WONDERLAND

Unit 36   Page 42

Words from Words: SCARCITY—act, arc, art, car, cart, cast, cat, city, cry, icy, sat, say, scar, scary, sir, sit, star, stay, sty, *and many more*

Unit 40   Page 46

Break the Code: ANYONE WHO CAN READ THIS DESERVES A SPECIAL TREAT.

Level C – Answers

Unit 41   Page 47

"omelet" (11-down) may also be spelled "omelette"

Words from Words: POACHING—aching, chain, chap, chin, china, chip, chop, coin, coping, gain, hang, hoping, icon, inch, pacing, pain, pang, panic, piano, pinch

Unit 42   Page 48

Anagram: 1-across, COMPETITION

Unit 43   Page 49

Words in Words: **A** ate (14-down, DATES) **B** cut (6-across, ACUTE ANGLES) **C** den (17-across, STUDENTS) **D** elf (8-across, ITSELF) **E** stern (9-down, EASTERN) **F** sure (16-across, MEASUREMENT) **G** tip (1-across, MULTIPLY)

Unit 44   Page 50

Anagrams: 9-across, tame → MEAT, MATE, TEAM; 10-across, dust → STUD; 3-down, site → TIES; 17-down, scar → CARS, ARCS

Unit 45   Page 51

Unit 46   Page 52

Check the Anagram: It is correct.

Word List

A

abacus
abuse
ached
aches
act
acted
actor
acts
acute angles
added
addict
address
admit
admitting
adult
adults
adverbs
advertising
afternoon
again
age
age group
aged
agreed
agreement
air
albatross
alibi
alligator
allow
almost
aloha
Alps
also
alter
altered
amber
amble
America
amount
ample
anchor
animal
answer
ant
Antarctica
anteaters
antecedents
antennas
antonym
ants
ape
apes
apologize
apple
arch
archer
arches
architects
archway
area
arguments
Aristotle
arm
aroma
aromas
arrested
arrow
arson
art
artery
artist
ash
Asia
asks
asleep
asps
asset
ate
Atlantic
atlas
attempt
attic
August
aunt
autumn
avenue
avenues
aviary

B

baboon
bad
bakery
banknotes
barbecue
basic
bass
battle
bed
beds
bee
beetle
Beirut
bell
bella
bellow
bill
billy goats
biped
birdbaths
birthdays
bisection
blinds
boasters
boiled
booklets
books
botanist
both
bough
bow
brain
branch
brave
breakers
breakfast
bridge
broom
brother
bud
buds
bugle
burglars
burns
bus
butter
byte
bytes

C

Cairo
calves
Canada
canal
cane
cannot
capacity
car
carrot
carton
cat
catch
census
cent
center
cheap
cheese
chef
cherry
chess
China
chocolates
chop
CIA
circle
citrus
clan
cliff
closer
clothes
clouds
coat hanger
comma
competition
computer
computers
conclusion
conductor
cones
conic
contestants
contract
coo
corner
cost
costs
costume
cot
cousin
cousins
cove
cow
cows
crawl
cream
crew
crop
crowds
cub
cups
cure
curtain

D

daddy
dads
damp
danger
dangerous
dashes
dates
decades
decay
deer
delta
deltas
den
denim
depots
desks
dictation
diets
digest
dinner
dirty
disappear
doctor
dollar
don't
donor
doors
doves
dozens
drag
dragon
drawings
drew
driftwood
drive
drop
drug
ducks
due
duet
dune
dust
duty

E

ear
early
earns
ears
earthworms
east
eastern
easy
eat
eaten
ebbs
echo
edge
eel
egg
Egypt
Egyptians
eight
eighty
elbow
elect
embark
emerald
emu
emus
ended
energy
enjoy
enter
entire
epic
eras
estate
Etna
Europe
even
event
Everest
ewe
ewes
exam
exams
except
exhales
extinct
extra
eyebrow
eyelid
eyes

F

fable
fact
facts
faded
false
family
famous
fare
farm
fast
fasten
fastest
fasts
father
Father Bear
fawns

Word List

feast
feathers
fed
felon
ferns
fever
fifth
fight
finals
fingers
finish
firefighter
fists
fixed
flat
flea
fleas
flies
flour
fog
forbid
forest
forks
fortnight
fruit

G

gander
gate
geese
gentle
germ
gift
glue
gluttony
goat
grapes
green grass
grip
grow
gum
gum tree
guru
gust

H

H_2O
habitat
half
hard
hare
Harry Potter
hated
hawk
health
height
help
helps
her
hesitate
high
hills
hip
his
hoe
hopped
horn
horse
horses
huge
hurls
hutches

I

ice
iced
icicle
idea
ideal
idle
igloo
igniting
ill
imprison
inch
independent
India
infinity
innocent
insects

inset
instep
intend
interesting
intestine
into
is not
island
isle
isolated
isosceles
italics
itchy
items
itself
ivy

J

jury

K

kernel
kettle
keyhole
kilogram
kilometer
kiwis
knob
knot
koala
koalas

L

labels
lake
lamb
lambs
latecomer
lately
later
Latin
lattice
lead
leaf
leap
learn

leek
length
leopard
less
let
lettuce
libraries
lie
likely
limp
linen
lion
lip
lipstick
lit
loaf
loses
lost
loudest

M

magic
magic wand
magnet
map
marinate
match
math
mathematics
mature
meal
meals
measurement
medal
mementos
menu
meteor
midweek
minus
miser
mist
moon
Mother Bear
mother-in-law
moths
multiply

mummy
museum
museums
music
myth
myths

N

narrate
native
navy
near
neat
need
nest
net
night
nil
nod
noise
nomadic
nonagons
note
noun
number line

O

oars
oasis
obey
obeyed
oblong
oboe
observer
obstacles
obtuse
ocean
octagon
odd
odors
off
ogre
ogres
omelet
omit
one

onion
onions
open
orange
orator
orbit
order
otter
outlaw
outside
oval
oven
ovens
over
owing
owl
oxen
oxygen

P

pact
padlocks
pal
panda
paper
Paris
parka
parrot
pasta
path
paw
pawpaw
pea
pear
pelicans
penguin
pepper
Peter
Peter Rabbit
phrase
pilot
pirates
plaid
plates
plus
poaching

poet
polo
pool
popcorn
porridge
port
posed
possum
potato
potatoes
power
prefer
prehistoric
premier
prime number
private
prize
pup
pups
purr
pyramid

Q

queers
queue
quiet
quilts
quite
quote

R

rain
rain forests
raked
ram
rare
rattlesnake
ray
reams
recipe
recommends
red
reefs
reign
remark
remembering

Word List

repayments
replied
reptile
result
returns
rhyme
rib
right angles
rim
rink
rip
ripe
roast
rob
robot
rock
rodent
roof
roses
rubella
rugby
ruined
run
runs
runs off
rural

S

sac
sad
sailor
salad
samurai
sand
sang
sap
saris
sausages
save
scar
scarcity
scared
scent
score
scraps
scream

scrub
scurvy
sea
sea level
seal
seas
seats
second
see
seed
seen
semi
sense
separates
serpent
sets
sews
shall
shallots
shark
shed
sheep
shell
shipyards
shoes
shop
shrub
shrug
shut
side
sides
sign
silent
sinks
sister
site
sits
ski
skin
skua
smash
smell
smile
smiles
smoke signal

snake
snap
snooze
snow
soar
sock
socks
SOS
sows
spa
speak
speed
speedboat
spend
sphinx
spiders
spin
spoons
staff
stag
stags
stamp
starting
starts
state
static
stay
steel
step
stepbrother
steps
stir
stoop
stop
strain
strong
students
sty
suddenly
summer
sunset
supermarket
sure
Susan
swarm

sweep
sweeping
swims
Swiss
syrups

T

table
tacks
talents
talkers
tall
tame
tamer
tarts
taste
tasted
taxi
tea
technology
teeth
telegrams
telephone
televisions
tell
ten
term
terminates
test
tests
their
thermometer
three
through
thumbs
ticks
tides
tie
tiger
tilt
timber
tiny
tiptoe
tire
tired
title

toad
toaster
today
Tom
tomato sauce
too
top
tortoise
toss
total
towel
toy
translator
transmit
transported
trapezoids
trees
trek
triangles
trim
trod
troll
truant
true
Tuesday
tulips
tuna
tusks
twelve
twists
two
typewriters

U

umbrella
uncle
under
unit
united
unlikely
unnecessary
until
untrue
uphill
use
used

user
users
uses
usual

V

valleys
vandals
Victoria
visitor

W

wallabies
warlock
was
wasps
watch
waterfall
wave
weep
wet
why
wigwams
wonderland
wrists

X

xyz

Y

yards
yawns
yeah
year
yes
yetis
you